Parenting the Challenging Child

Parenting the Challenging Child

THE 4-STEP WAY TO TURN PROBLEM SITUATIONS INTO LEARNING OPPORTUNITIES

LIFE SPACE CRISIS INTERVENTION
Turning Problem Situations into Learning Opportunities

www.lsci.org

© 2019 LSCI Institute
www.lsci.org

All rights reserved. No part of the material protected by this copyright notice may be reproduced or used in any form or by any means, electronic or mechanical, including photocopying, recording, or by any information storage and retrieval system, without prior written permission of the copyright owner.

ISBN 978-0-578-46249-3

Layout Design: Melissa Payne

Printed in the United States of America by Specialty Printing and Marketing.

This book is dedicated to Dr. J.C. Chambers, the inspiring LSCI trainer, colleague, and friend whose dedication to bringing LSCI concepts to parents and caregivers was the driving force behind this book.

—Signe Whitson

Contents

Preface — 9
What Is the Life Space Crisis Intervention Approach?

CHAPTER 1 — 19
Turn Conflict Situations Into Learning Opportunities
The 3 Foundations of LSCI

CHAPTER 2 — 33
The Importance of a Drain-Off Period
How to Soothe a Stressed-Out Child

CHAPTER 3 — 39
Building a Timeline
Putting Language to Emotion

CHAPTER 4 — 55
The 4-Step Process
Drain Off, Timeline, Understanding the Problem, and Skill Building

CHAPTER 5 — 71
The SOS Intervention
Identifying the Real Source of the Stress

CHAPTER 6 — 91
The Reality Check Intervention
Clarifying Perceptions of Reality

Contents

115   CHAPTER 7
The New Tools Intervention
Teaching New Social Skills

137   CHAPTER 8
The Encouraging Empathy Intervention
Confronting Unacceptable Behavior

157   CHAPTER 9
The Strengthening Self-Control Intervention
Helping Kids Overcome Impulsivity and Guilt

179   CHAPTER 10
The Setup Intervention
Resisting Manipulation in Sibling and Peer Relationships

201   CHAPTER 11
Parenting the Challenging Child
Resources to Help Manage the Challenging Behaviors of Your Children and Adolescents

211   References

PREFACE

What Is the Life Space Crisis Intervention Approach?

Life Space Crisis Intervention (LSCI) is a set of skills that helps parents and caregivers turn problem situations into learning opportunities for young people. LSCI views adult–child conflicts as occasions for skill development, relationship building, and positive behavioral changes.

Since 1991, the LSCI Institute has trained more than 100,000 professionals from the fields of education, psychology, social work, counseling, and Child and Youth Care (CYC) to understand that the problems kids cause are not the causes of their problems . To genuinely reach and effectively teach young people, the Institute provides both an overall philosophy and a practical framework that guide adult interactions with challenging children.

> **The problems kids cause are not the causes of their problems.** —Dr. Nicholas J. Long

Based on requests from our participants, the LSCI Institute developed this resource—in addition to two live training opportunities—to adapt its brain-based, trauma-informed, kid-centered approach to the unique needs of parents and caregivers. *Parenting the Challenging Child* provides readers with the following:

- An understanding of what is happening in a young person's brain during a stressful situation

- Practical strategies to calm stressed-out children and help them begin to talk about their perceptions, thoughts, feelings, and behaviors

- Specific skills for listening and asking questions that guide kids to better understand problem behavior

- Realistic ideas that help young people begin to change destructive behavior patterns

- A consistent, step-by-step framework for intervening in problem situations and turning them into learning opportunities

After reading this solution-focused book, you will be equipped with new knowledge and skills to identify six problematic patterns of behavior in young people and implement a consistent 4-step verbal process to address and change each one. Even more importantly, you will learn about yourself and how simple changes in the way you interact with your loved ones during a problem situation can significantly improve your relationship and their future behaviors.

Improving Your Relationship With Your Child

Throughout this book, we will share many real-life examples and situations to shed light on how the LSCI approach works. In the example that follows, you will see what happens when LSCI is not used and a parent misses an opportunity to use a school-based problem as a skill-building experience.

The Situation

> *Just as Dylan arrived home from school, his mother was hanging up the phone from a conversation with his science teacher. The mother was feeling furious after hearing about Dylan's reported refusal to participate in class. When Dylan walked in the front door, his mother grabbed his cell phone from his hand and told him he was grounded for two weeks. Before sending him to his room, she yelled at him for having the nerve to reach into his teacher's desk drawer.*

> *What Dylan's mother did not know—and failed to ask about—was that just before science, a classmate had taken Dylan's science project out of his backpack and hidden it under the teacher's desk. The whole class laughed and taunted Dylan as he searched the room to find it. He was humiliated. When his teacher saw him rummaging about the classroom, she yelled at him in front of everyone and refused to listen to his explanation of why he was out of his seat in the first place.*

There are three possible outcomes to any adult–child conflict (Long, Wood, & Fecser, 2001):

Parent–Child Relationship Unchanged

An adult's immediate reaction to a problem situation with a child is often punishment. Many parents have a go-to set of "consequences" they use with their kids. For many young people, however, these rote punishments have little effect on changing behavior because they address only the symptoms and not the perceptions, thoughts, and feelings that underlie the behavior. As a result, nothing really changes except that the likelihood of future problems increases.

In the example above, Dylan's mother responded angrily to her son—yelling at him, taking his cell phone, grounding him, and sending him to his room. Although these may be routine consequences for misbehavior in Dylan's family, they fail to teach Dylan any of the skills he needs to prevent the problem from happening again. What's more, the mother has no insight or understanding into why her son behaved this way in the first place. An opportunity for mutual understanding between the parent and child was completely missed.

Parent–Child Relationship Damaged

As parents, we have a lot on our plates on a daily basis. From our own busy and stress-filled lives to managing the inevitable highs and lows of a young person's day, we are often quick to speak and slow to listen. When a problem arises, our instinct is to quickly solve it. Although efficiency is often valued in our fast-paced lives, whenever we address a surface behavior without understanding its cause, we run the risk of making matters worse.

Sometimes our spontaneous reactions even cause pain to the very people we are trying to help. In our hurry or frustration, we may unintentionally humiliate, degrade, or belittle our loved ones. Over time, resentment builds and our children begin to feel rejected. This alienation breeds mistrust and practically guarantees that conflicts will continue.

By rushing to judgment in the example above, Dylan's mother ran the risk of causing real damage to her relationship with her son. Dylan is a young man who already had the experience of being humiliated by his peers that day in school and felt disregarded by his teacher when he tried to explain his situation. By quickly punishing him and failing to first listen to his side of the story, the mother became the third source of alienation and rejection her son experienced that day and likely confirmed his belief that others are cruel and untrustworthy.

Parent–Child Relationship Improved

When we address kids' misbehaviors (e.g., disrespect, yelling, cursing, rule breaking) but fail to understand what is causing those behaviors, we make problems worse. ***Parenting the Challenging Child* offers a consistent, 4-step process that can turn that around.** In this book, you will learn practical strategies to take you past rigid discipline and toward a more effective way to relate to your child. The LSCI approach can help you and your child build a relationship based on mutual understanding and genuine trust, which leads to lasting changes in perceptions, thoughts, feelings, and behaviors.

Had the mother been equipped with LSCI knowledge and skills, she could have handled the situation in a far more positive way. Rather than rushing to punish Dylan, she would have used a specific set of Drain-Off and Timeline skills (thoroughly described in Chapters 2 and 3) to hear Dylan's side of the story. Then, based on this information, she could have helped him understand where things went wrong (Chapter 3) and what to do differently in future situations to prevent a similar problem (Chapter 4). Through the LSCI process, Dylan's trust in his mother and knowledge of how to handle peer manipulation would both have increased.

How to Use This Book

Through the first four chapters of this book, you will learn the foundational skills of LSCI. Then, in Chapters 5–10, you will learn how to apply these core skills to six of the most common problematic behavioral patterns demonstrated by children and adolescents. LSCI's 4-step process provides you with a Parenting GPS of sorts, giving you step-by-step guidance for how to de-escalate stressful situations, listen effectively, ask the right questions, arrive at helpful insights, teach your child new skills, and most importantly, strengthen your relationship with your child.

We hope you will read this book in order, learning first the foundational skills of LSCI and then how to apply them to specific patterns of behavior. We also realize that your time is precious and you may be focused on a very specific problem behavior. Our recommendation for best meeting the needs and goals that caused you to select this book is to read the first four chapters in order, as they are universal principles that apply to almost any challenging parenting situation. Likewise, a careful read of Chapter 5 ("The SOS Intervention: Identifying the Real Source of Stress") should precede reading other chapters for the following main reasons:

1. The Source of Stress (SOS) intervention tends to be the most frequently used intervention among parents with aggressive or emotionally reactive kids.

2. Because it is the first of the Intervention chapters, the SOS section offers the most comprehensive details on how to effectively carry out the 4-step process.

We do hope that you find every page and chapter of this book to be filled with practical ideas and strategies. We know that theory is important, but what parents and caregivers really want when they pick up a book is easy-to-understand, easy-to-apply strategies to help their loved ones. We hope we have met this objective. Please visit us online at **www.lsci.org** for additional information about the LSCI approach.

In closing, we want to emphasize that the LSCI process is simple, but it is not easy. Parenting is an incredibly demanding and difficult responsibility. Just when we think we have our children figured out, they grow and change and do something that takes us completely by surprise. That's why LSCI is so powerful. It gives us a framework for understanding what's going on in a child's brain (no matter what may be coming out of his mouth!) and offers us a system for responding in a way that builds a more positive relationship while teaching more effective behaviors.

The LSCI process is simple, but it is not easy.

Continue reading for a brief history of LSCI.

A Brief History of Life Space Crisis Intervention (LSCI)

The LSCI approach for helping young people has a long and rich history that is grounded in the works of several prominent thought leaders in the fields of psychology, social work, education, and youth care. We trace our roots to the founder of psychoanalysis himself, Sigmund Freud. Freud was the first person to recognize that there is an unconscious part of the mind that drives feelings and that those feelings can be expressed as specific behaviors. As you will read in Chapter 1, LSCI is a strategy that helps parents and caregivers look beyond behavior to find out what's driving it.

Freud's daughter, Anna, was well known for her work in child psychology. Anna Freud also theorized that there are ways people unconsciously deal with stress and that if these ways become repetitive patterns, they can become destructive.

Fritz Redl, an Austrian-born man originally trained by Anna, emigrated to the United States in the 1930s where he developed a distinguished career as a child psychologist and teacher. Redl worked with troubled adolescents throughout his career. In the 1940s, he partnered with a social worker named David Wineman.

Redl and Wineman believed that adults who interact regularly with young people—as opposed to during appointment-based sessions in a therapist's office—have the greatest opportunity to help kids make lasting behavioral changes. We believe that parents are in this unique position to have a profound influence on their children. Redl and Wineman developed a process that evolved into the "Life Space Interview" (LSI).

In 1952, while Redl and Wineman were working in Detroit, 60 miles northwest a man named William Morse established the University of Michigan's Fresh Air Camp. The camp became a renowned interdisciplinary training center for psychiatry, psychology, social work, and special education, with LSI taught as a major therapeutic strategy. Nicholas Long, a graduate student of Morse, received his initial LSI training at the Fresh Air Camp.

Over the next four decades, further development of LSI occurred under the direction of Morse and Long. Its use was extended into the educational environment where it could be used by teachers. In 1971, Nicholas Long founded the Rose School in Washington D.C., a community-based psychoeducational program that served some of the most troubled children in the city. Hundreds of clinicians and educators used LSI with thousands of young people at the Rose School.

During the early 1990s, Long began developing a model for LSI training. With Frank Fecser, CEO of Positive Education Program in Cleveland, Ohio, the two designed and piloted several professional training programs. With Fecser and Mary Wood, founder of the Developmental Therapy Center in Athens, Georgia, Long authored *Life Space Crisis Intervention: Talking With Students in Conflict*. Life Space Intervention became "Life Space Crisis Intervention" to reflect its application in stressful situations.

Since 1991, more than 100,000 professionals have been trained in the skills of LSCI across the United States, Canada, Europe, Australia, New Zealand, and beyond. As a result, well over 1 million young people have benefited from this skill-building, relationship-improving approach.

In 2014, as the Institute began offering training that adapted its approach to the unique needs of parents and caregivers, the Parents Division of the LSCI Institute was established. Now, we offer these skills to you through this one-of-a-kind book. We hope you find LSCI skills to be a game-changer in terms of improving your relationship with your child, increasing your knowledge of what happens in the brain during stressful situations, better understanding the dynamics of conflict, and helping your child turn problem situations into learning opportunities.

CHAPTER 1

TURN CONFLICT SITUATIONS INTO LEARNING OPPORTUNITIES
The 3 Foundations of LSCI

FOUNDATION 1:
Nurturing a Positive Relationship With Your Child

The importance of positive relationships in a young person's life can never be overstated. Through warm, supportive, and trusting relationships with parents and caregivers, kids gain the strength they need to overcome problems and bounce back from life's challenges. What's more, caring, consistent relationships offer the structure and support they need to make lasting changes in their behavior. When a child perceives that the adults in his life are truly invested in his well-being and interested in his experiences, he is more willing to talk about what is going on in his life and more likely to be open to adult feedback.

In the Preface to this book, it is noted that the LSCI approach to helping kids is simple but not always easy. Likewise, the most meaningful connections adults make with kids are usually based on the simplest of gestures. A smile, a word of reassurance, a bit of your undivided attention, a thoughtful response, an opportunity to practice a new skill, a hug just when it is needed most—all of these supportive behaviors are at once free and priceless. Each of them communicates to a young person that she has worth and value. Every kindness builds the relationship between the parent and child.

So, what's not easy about that?

In our years of offering LSCI training, one of the most common hesitations we hear from participants is something along the lines of, *"This approach is great! I wish adults would have used LSCI with me when I was a kid. But things are different today.*

Life is so busy. I don't know how I'd ever have time to sit down with my child and have an LSCI conversation."

Before we get any further into this book, we want to tell you that using the LSCI approach with young people is tremendously helpful—and it takes time. LSCI is not a quick, once-and-done, magic wand solution to all parenting problems. It is a *systematic, relationship-building* approach to helping your child build *self-regulation* and *problem-solving skills.* Some LSCI conversations happen in 10 minutes. Some take more like 20. If you are in the car and taking your time processing an incident with your child, your LSCI chat could go on for as long as a half-hour. Although there is no set schedule in which an LSCI conversation occurs, authentic relationships and lasting learning are built over time, and giving your time to your child is another foundation of LSCI.

Give Your Time

Time is a great equalizer. We all have just 24 hours in a day. It's doubtful we have met a single parent or caregiver who feels like 24 hours is enough time to accomplish all of their tasks. And yet this is all the time that any of us are given. How will we make the most of time when it comes to parenting our kids?

With apologies, we have to admit that LSCI does not offer suggestions or solutions for adding hours to your day. What we do offer is the idea that, as adults responsible for the well-being of young people, we have to be willing to put our to-do lists to the side every once in a while, especially when a child asks for our help. For better or for worse, it is certain that the to-do list items will still be there waiting for us when we come back around to them. Kids, on the other hand, don't always linger after an adult has ignored or dismissed them. We're stuck with our tasks until they are completed, but our kids grow up—and grow away—very quickly.

Is Time Enough?

Can all parent–child problems be resolved simply through the gift of time? No. Of course not. For some young people, the support and intervention needed from adults goes beyond just the minutes on a clock. On the other hand, something as simple and uncomplicated as a supportive 10-minute conversation from a parent can go a surprisingly long way in helping a young person think more rationally, make better decisions, and feel less of the alienation that prompted previous misbehaviors.

What Happens If I Don't Give Time?

When kids feel alienated from parents and caregivers, we all have a lot to worry about. This statement applies to acts of youth aggression and poor behavior across the board. Without strong adult connections, young people feel isolated from sources of support and act without the hindrance of disapproval by an adult who matters to them (Whitson, 2014).

For those who still are thinking "there is not enough time in the day" to connect with young people in need, know that your child will get your time one way or the other. It may be in positive ways, or it may be through acting out and creating crisis situations. The question is, How do you want to spend your time with your child? A proactive investment of your time using LSCI to talk with a young person about a problem situation is a whole lot simpler than picking up the pieces after an angry, violent, destructive outburst.

> Your child will get your time one way or the other. The question is, How do you want to spend your time with your child?

What Do Positive Relationships Have to Do With the LSCI Approach?

James Comer (1995) put it well: *"No significant learning occurs without a significant relationship."* The LSCI approach uses the positive relationships between parents and children to help young people learn, grow, and make lasting changes in their perceptions, thoughts, feelings, and behaviors. When used consistently to process problem situations, LSCI gives kids the skills they need to put language to their emotions, make sense out of chaotic events, understand how their actions contributed to a problem situation, and learn new skills to prevent or avoid the same thing from happening all over again.

FOUNDATION 2:
How to Soothe the Brain and Ready Kids for Conversation

In order to effectively guide young people through problem situations, it is essential to begin with a basic understanding of how the human brain responds to stress and perceived danger. In the 1960s, the neuroscientist Paul MacLean introduced the concept of the triune brain, a simplified but very helpful model that focuses on the interaction of three specific regions of the human brain during stressful events. For our purposes, we summarize MacLean's model as follows:

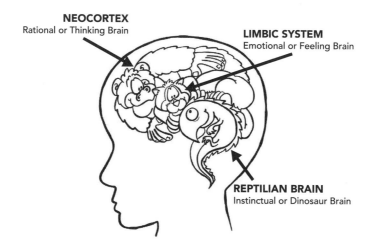

The Brainstem

From an evolutionary perspective, the oldest part of the human brain is called the brainstem. Also known as the *reptilian brain*, this part of the brain (that still dominates the overall behavior of creatures like snakes and lizards) controls human survival functions, such as breathing, heart rate, and balance. A key feature of the *brainstem* is that it does not learn well from experience but rather repeats instinctual behaviors over and over in a fixed way (Baars & Gage, 2010).

Applying knowledge of the brainstem to our interactions with kids helps us understand that when the brainstem is activated, a child's heart may automatically race, her breathing may instinctively quicken, and/or her blood pressure may suddenly rise, causing her face to flush or her body to feel uncomfortable. All of these physical responses are automatic and beyond a child's active control. They are the brain's natural way of preparing the body to protect itself from danger—which is essential for survival.

The Limbic System

Layered over the brainstem is the mammalian brain, often referred to as the *limbic system* or, in simplest terms, the *emotional brain*. The limbic system directs the human body's emotional responses. **Developmentally, young people's brains tend to be dominated by the limbic system.** When adults causally remark that a child seems to be driven by their emotions, they are usually quite correct.

> Fight, flight, and freeze reactions are all brain-directed, instinctual responses rather than purposeful, willful, or intentionally defiant acts.

This limbic system includes the amygdala, an almond-shaped structure that is responsible for the body's *fight, flight, or freeze* response. We will refer to the amygdala and "amygdala-driven responses" often throughout this book. In practical terms, when the amygdala perceives any kind of danger, it directs the body to either fight the threat (e.g., through yelling, physical aggression), flee the situation (e.g., by running away, withdrawal), or freeze up (e.g., shutting down emotionally). Fight, flight, and freeze reactions are all brain-directed, instinctual responces rather than purposeful, willful, or intentionally defiant acts.

A critically important feature of the limbic system is that *this part of the brain does not have access to words and language.* When activated by a perceived threat, the limbic system is not able to communicate with the parts of the brain responsible for language or even logic. Below, we will talk about why this separation of feelings from language and logic is so significant and explain how the LSCI approach helps bridge this critical gap.

The brainstem and limbic system work closely together. When the amygdala perceives a threat in the environment, it activates the survival functions of the brainstem. Together, these parts of the brain adhere to the "better safe than sorry" principle, activating survival functions and flight/flight/freeze responses anytime they detect a threat, without necessarily evaluating the nature of the threat. Have you ever jumped when you saw something coiled in the grass, only to realize it is a garden hose rather than a snake? That's your amygdala talking.

The Neocortex

The neocortex, or the *thinking brain*, as it is commonly called, is the part of the brain that kicks in to remind you that you left the hose out earlier in the day and that you don't need to fight the "coiled figure" or run away from it.

The neocortex is involved in "higher" brain functions, such as evaluating, problem solving, reasoning, planning, logical thinking, and language. Developmentally, the neocortex is not fully mature until a person is in his twenties. It is not surprising then—nor should it be the mark of a "problem" child—that kids need consistent adult intervention and guidance to be able to fully access the logical, rational, thinking part of their brain.

It is also worth noting that, whereas adult brains typically are dominated by the neocortex, we, too, in times of stress, can have what is known as an "amygdala hijack" (Goleman, 2005) and revert to behaviors that are driven by our emotional brains. An important part of the Conflict Cycle™ (see Foundation 3, below) is the management of our own responses to a child's troubling behaviors and making sure that we control our reactions in a rational way rather than an amygdala-driven, conflict-fueling one.

Applying the Triune Brain Model to the LSCI Approach

As noted above, *the limbic system does not have access to words and language*. It is critical for parents and caregivers to be aware that, when a young person's body is instinctively gearing up to deal with a stressful situation, it is unable to put language to all of this emotion.

> When a young person's body is instinctively gearing up to deal with a stressful situation, it is unable to put language to all of this emotion.

As adults, we want (and often demand) that kids "use their words" to tell us what they are upset about. Having an understanding of the limbic system's dominance over a young person's brain activity during a stressful situation helps us understand why, in the heat of the moment, kids *lack the ability*—not the will—to put words to how they are feeling. This basic understanding of how a young person's brain functions is critical because it helps us, as parents, adjust our expectations and accept that kids are doing the best they can with the brains they have.

LSCI is an approach that helps parents and caregivers soothe the overactive emotional brain (using the skills of Drain Off, covered in Chapter 2) and bring language to emotion (using the Timeline skills described in Chapter 3) so that kids are better able to access their neocortex and utilize the problem-solving part of their brain. *With LSCI, our goal is always to move kids' raw perceptions, thoughts, and feelings from the part of the brain that doesn't have language to the part of the brain that does.* In doing so, we help kids begin to understand the destructive nature of their behaviors and learn skills to deal with problems.

FOUNDATION 3:
Understanding the LSCI Conflict Cycle

The LSCI Conflict Cycle

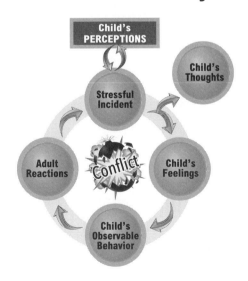

The third foundation of LSCI is the Conflict Cycle. The LSCI Conflict Cycle explains the circular and escalating dynamics of conflict between parents and children and offers important insights about the parent's role in either fueling problem situations or halting them before they spiral out of control.

To get a rich understanding of the Conflict Cycle, we will begin by considering how adults and children typically perceive, think, feel, and behave in response to stressful events and problem situations. An awareness of these elements of the Conflict Cycle will give us important insights into why kids sometimes behave in troubling ways.

26 • Chapter 1

Perception

In general, adults know there are many ways to perceive the world. For example, if we were to look at the image below, some of us would see a duck and some of us would see a rabbit. Hopefully, when asked to consider if the other perception was valid, we would acknowledge that, although our point of view is accurate, the other person's point of view is also correct. Based on our life experiences, we can acknowledge that other people's points of view have merit and that two people can have opposing ways of looking at the world and still both be "right."

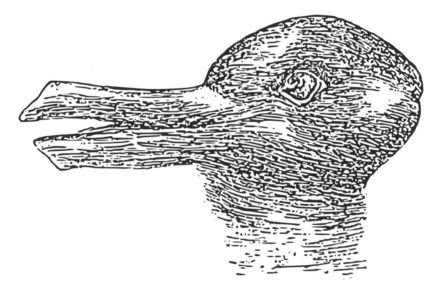

We also know that stress can heavily influence our perceptions when it comes to the way we look at problem situations. As a result, we are usually willing to listen to alternative viewpoints. Sometimes we even reconsider our own!

Young people often have a much more difficult time accepting alternate points of view. In times of stress, kids can become especially concrete about their perceptions. Parents and caregivers can make the mistake of believing that their kids are simply being stubborn when they insist that their perception of an event is the only correct one. The idea that the child "knows the truth about what happened but won't admit it" can trigger a hostile reaction from adults. *At this point, both the adult and the child are perceiving each other from a place of hostility.*

> To carry out the LSCI process, it is essential for parents and caregivers to recognize the following:
>
> 1. We all have unique ways of perceiving our world. Knowing how a child perceives a situation is always the starting point for teaching an alternate perception. We have to make time to find out how the child perceives an event before we can offer new information.
>
> 2. A child's ability to consider other points of view has to do with the availability and approachability of an adult who will listen and dialog with the child.
>
> 3. Parents and children both enter conflict situations with a sense of being "right." Insisting that the other person change his point of view usually only results in increased hostility and defensiveness about the original position.
>
> The LSCI approach offers a solution to the tendency of adults and kids to become locked in rigid and opposing ways of perceiving an event.

Thinking and Feeling

In our earlier discussion of the second foundation of LSCI ("How to Soothe the Brain and Ready Kids for Conversation"), we thoroughly examined the brain-based origins of stressed-out thoughts and overwhelming feelings. The Conflict Cycle paradigm shows us how the perceived stress of an event can trigger a set of amygdala-driven thoughts and feelings which, in turn, drive a young person's unwanted or unacceptable behaviors.

Behavior

As we look at each individual component of the Conflict Cycle, it is important to note that behavior is usually the first part that gets our attention. There are no flashing lights to warn a parent about an alarming set of perceptions or an amygdala-driven cluster of thoughts and feelings in a child. Rather, it is usually a disruptive behavior(s) that first makes us aware of a problem.

It's also important for parents and caregivers to think of their child's poor behavior as a *symptom*. Behavior is a reflection of the unique perceptions, thoughts, and feelings the child is experiencing over a particular event. LSCI challenges traditional thinking about why kids show unwanted behavior. We often hear that kids act out because they want power, control, or attention. It's true that we all want some power and control over our environment. Most of us crave some attention and human interaction. These are good things. If children didn't want them, we'd really be worried about them. As illogical as it might seem, the problems that kids create are usually an attempt to gain some power, control, or attention. What's more, their acting up and acting out is rarely just random. Usually, it is predictable (Fecser, 2013). If you think of your child who challenges you the most, you can probably predict with a good deal of accuracy what kind of problem he's going to get into next. Most kids behave in repetitive patterns.

Knowledge of the LSCI Conflict Cycle guides parents and caregivers to understand how certain stressful situations trigger predictable perceptions, thoughts, feelings, and unwanted behaviors. *If we can predict it, we can prevent it.* In other words, adults can use the Conflict Cycle as a roadmap to *anticipate* troubling behavior and *intervene* to help kids develop more positive ways of thinking and better coping skills to deal with overwhelming feelings. Over time, consistent use of the LSCI approach helps parents *prevent* the troubling behavior from occurring again and again.

In Chapters 5–10, you will learn about six specific patterns of self-defeating behavior and gain skills for using the LSCI process—with the Conflict Cycle as your guide—to help kids change patterns of destructive behavior.

Adult Response

As parents and caregivers, if we are not thoughtful, purposeful, and aware, we will react to a child's poor behavior as if it is occurring in isolation—forgetting that there is a whole set of perceptions, thoughts, and feelings that drive it. We may resort to rote punishment or hurtful, impulsive responses that damage our relationship with our child.

Keep in mind: The adult's response is the only element of the Conflict Cycle parents have any control over. If our ultimate goal is to teach young people that they have choices when it comes to their behavior, we must begin by role modeling positive choices of our own, particularly in terms of how we respond to our kids' unwanted behaviors.

> **The adult's responce is the only element of the Conflict Cycle parents have any control over.**

Read the real-life example below of one parent's effective response to her child's challenging behavior.

A parent arrived at school to pick up her fourth-grade daughter for a scheduled doctor's appointment. As the daughter approached her mother in the school hallway, she began to cry and yell, "I don't want to go! This always happens. You always make me leave!"

The mother could feel the stares of her daughter's teacher as well as the school nurse and counselor, who were all witnessing the situation. She felt the pressure of their judgment both on her parenting and on her loud, disruptive child. She realized right away that she had two choices:

1. She could use a traditional disciplinary approach and firmly tell her daughter to quiet down in the hallway and stop her disrespect immediately.

She felt justified that this would be an appropriate parental response, but she also knew that for her daughter, this would have been the next stressful event and would have triggered even more upsetting thoughts and feelings in the emotional part of her daughter's brain. Things would have gotten worse for sure.

2. Option 2 was to try to tap into her daughter's rational brain in an effort to get more of a logical response.

First, she got down on her daughter's level and hugged her. She said, "You are really upset right now." Her daughter took one long sob and then melted into her mother's arms.

Just at that moment, the school nurse, who had heard all of the commotion in the hallway, joined in the conversation with a well-intentioned but too quick rational brain response: "Your mom is trying to keep you healthy. What would happen if you didn't get a flu shot?" she asked. The child stiffened and started crying and yelling at her mother all over again.

Her mother gave her time. She continued to hug her. She wiped her tears. She used validating words instead of becoming defensive: "You feel like I am picking you up from school too early, and you are missing your recess time with your friends. This happened last month too, and you are feeling sad all over again."

The child softened and made eye contact with her mother. She nodded and said, "Yes, I am so sad."

Within two minutes of this soothing interaction with her mother, the young girl regained her composure. As she walked out of the building, she was respectful, relieved, and ready to go to her doctor's appointment.

In this situation, Option 1 may have been appropriate, but it would have been a missed opportunity for the parent to connect and communicate with her child and help her daughter practice skills for calming down and connecting language to emotion.

Does that mean a parent should allow her child to "get away with" the disrespectful behavior that was initially displayed in the school hallway? No. There is a time for setting standards and communicating with young people about acceptable behaviors—but this parent used her knowledge of the LSCI Conflict Cycle as a roadmap to understand that it would be more effective to wait to address these important issues when her child was more in control and more receptive to learning.

The LSCI Conflict Cycle

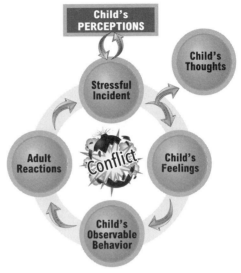

Understandably, troubling behaviors by a child—especially those that seem to come "out of the blue"—can create big reactions in adults, and we don't all respond as well as this mother did. Unfortunately, too often parents take on a child's feelings and even mirror the child's behaviors. They may raise their voices, threaten punishment, or say hurtful things. This negative adult reaction, in turn, becomes the next stressful event for the child and creates a new turn of a Conflict Cycle . Self-defeating power struggles between parents and children continue to ensue. Understanding the Conflict Cycle is the first line of defense against reinforcing a child's irrational beliefs and engaging in these no-win dynamics.

SUMMARY

Even parents and kids with the most positive of relationships get into Conflict Cycles sometimes. Effective parenting is not the absence of conflict entirely but rather knowledge of how stressful situations can activate the emotional part of the brain and prevent kids (and adults!) from using their thinking brains to effectively manage the conflict.

The LSCI Conflict Cycle offers a visual guide to understand—and therefore help prevent—escalating power struggles between parents and children. In the next two chapters, you will learn the LSCI skills needed to help you de-escalate the intense thoughts and feelings that can be triggered by stressful situations. Ultimately, you will learn new ways to effectively disengage from no-win conflicts with kids. The goal of LSCI is to make young people feel safe and supported enough to choose to talk about their feelings with a parent rather than to act them out in disruptive or destructive ways.

CHAPTER 2

THE IMPORTANCE OF A DRAIN-OFF PERIOD:
How to Soothe a Stressed-Out Child

In LSCI, we use the term *Drain Off* to describe the process of helping a young person regain control over his brain's amygdala-driven responses and begin to access his neocortex in order to put language to his emotions. (See Chapter 1 for a thorough review of "How to Soothe the Brain and Ready Kids for Conversation.") Drain-Off skills are effective anytime a child is experiencing stress. They are an essential tool for preventing escalating Conflict Cycles and building trust between a caregiver and child.

The skills of Drain Off include five core ways to listen to young people and speak in ways that soothe and "drain off" their intense emotions.

1. Attending Skills

Attending skills communicate that you are there to listen, are attentive to your child's needs, and want to hear what she has to say. The skill of attending is done through words, actions, and even silence.

Attending phrases:

- *I want to hear what you have to say.*
- *You seem to be starting to relax a little—that's great.*
- *Can I get you some water?*
- *Would you like to sit in this chair or over there?*
- *It can be so hard to talk when you're feeling angry. Let's take some deep breaths together so you can begin to feel better.*
- *Soon, we'll walk through what happened so I can really understand your point of view.*

Attending actions:
- *Making gentle eye contact*
- *Standing or sitting at the young person's eye level*
- *Positive, engaged facial expression*
- *Nonthreatening tone of voice*
- *Genuine interest in the child's point of view*

The purposeful and caring use of silence is another vital attending behavior that assists in draining off a young person's intense emotions. Silence makes some adults feel uneasy—like they are not doing enough. In their well-intended rush to solve a problem, adults often talk more than they listen and fill up any quiet space with words. Although this section of the book offers you many suggestions for effective words and phrases to soothe a child in distress, bear in mind that *sometimes saying nothing is preferable to saying something.* The simple, wordless presence of a supportive adult can be immensely calming to a young person.

> **The simple, wordless presence of a supportive adult can be immensely calming to a young person.**

2. Reassuring Skills

Reassuring skills let your child know that you care about her and are interested in the issues that are important to her. Effective reassurance communicates that you want to help solve the problem and an optimism that, together, you and your child can figure out what to do. Reassuring statements that can help drain off a child's intense emotions include:

- *I am here to help.*
- *I want to understand things from your point of view.*
- *We can figure this out together.*
- *We're going to work this out.*
- *It takes a lot of courage to talk about what you are thinking and feeling.*

3. Affirming Skills

Affirming skills communicate to a young person that you value him and believe there is a better side of him than his problem behavior. Helpful affirming statements include:

- *Thank you for being willing to sit here with me quietly.*
- *I like the way you're starting to use words.*
- *You're doing a great job settling down and getting ready to talk.*
- *You are handling a difficult situation really well.*
- *I can see that was hard for you to say. I'm proud of you.*

4. Validating Skills

Validating skills let a young person know that you nonjudgmentally accept his thoughts, feelings, and behaviors as important and understandable. A helpful validating statement often puts a child's emotional state into words, a brain-based strategy that helps move him toward engaging his neocortex. Examples of effective validating statements include:

- *I can see that you are angry with me.*
- *It sounds like you felt very uncomfortable.*
- *You are feeling frustrated that your brother won't let you have a turn.*
- *I can understand you are feeling embarrassed about what happened.*
- *That must have been a really scary situation.*

5. Decoding Skills

Decoding skills help kids connect their outward behaviors to what they are feeling inside. Decoding your child's emotions allows him to feel heard and understood which, in turn, helps him feel more relaxed and therefore better able to engage his thinking brain. Examples of effective decoding statements include:

- *Throwing the book told me that you were frustrated, and that's really important information for me. It's OK to just tell me this in words next time.*

- *It made you sad when you had to stay home with the babysitter. Cursing was your way to show me that you were upset.*

- *Lying about how the table got broken was your way of protecting your little sister. I am happy that you are looking out for her but need to know that you will always be honest with me no matter what happened.*

The Caregiver's Role in Using Drain-Off Skills

Listening to young people in a way that helps them calm down and begin to think clearly is a relatively *simple* skill. With supportive body language, encouraging words, and the soothing use of silence, the skill of de-escalating a problem situation can be mastered by most people.

What makes the skill of Drain Off *difficult* for some parents and caregivers is the challenge it poses to maintain their calm and stay in their own thinking brain even when they are on the receiving end of their child's emotional display. Angry feelings, vulgar language, and unacceptable behaviors are very often present at the start of a problem situation. If parents are not careful, they will mirror their child's emotional behavior and accidentally ignite the conflict they were hoping to extinguish.

As noted in Chapter 1, the parent's response is the only part of the Conflict Cycle we have any control over. In the heat of a problem situation, our job is to act on what is best for our child instead of reacting based on our own angry feelings or aggressive impulses. Long, Wood, and Fecser (2001) remind caring adults to act like a thermostat that actively turns down the heat on a conflict rather than like a thermometer that unwittingly reflects the child's temperature during a problem.

> Lastly, notice that in this chapter on the skills of Drain Off, there is no mention of making time to confront a child's lies, prove the adult's point, discuss punishment, or even get around to solving the problem. Rest assured, all of the steps necessary to successfully resolve the conflict are part of the LSCI process and will happen in due time. To be effective, however, the first step of an LSCI conversation is reserved solely for draining off the young person's intense emotions.

The parent's response is the only part of the Conflict Cycle we have any control over.

---

9 Skills for Becoming a Better Listener

Effective listening is the key to helping children regain control of the irrational thoughts and explosive feelings that occur during periods of stress. In LSCI, listening is much more than just a physical act of hearing. It is a set of intentional, planned, patient skills that allow a child to feel heard and understood. It is the basis for establishing a trusting relationship and essential for both preventing problems from escalating and de-escalating stressful situations that have already begun.

Summarized below are nine specific ways parents and caregivers can improve their ability to listen well to children who are experiencing distress and exhibiting behavioral problems.

1. **Really want to listen:** Almost all problems in listening can be overcome by an adult truly valuing what a child has to say.

2. **Listen to understand:** Don't just listen to hear a child's words. Aim to really understand what is being said.

3. **Stop talking:** You can't listen while you are talking. In a conversation, let the child finish what he is saying before you begin to speak.

4. **Concentrate on what the young person is saying:** Avoid planning your next comment while the child is talking.

5. **React appropriately:** Use body language to respond to important information or funny comments.

6. **Make eye contact:** Look at the child while he is speaking. Don't stare the child down, but definitely signal that you are paying attention.

7. **Don't have mental arguments about what the child is saying:** It will show on your face and set up unwanted barriers.

8. **Don't judge:** Wait until all the facts are given before you make a judgment on the child's message.

9. **Ask questions:** When you don't understand, when you need further clarification, and/or when you want to show you are listening, ask questions.

FROM DRAIN OFF TO TIMELINE

How we listen to kids is critical. When we're listening, we're always trying to link emotions and language. The five core listening skills of attending, reassuring, affirming, validating, and decoding help parents and caregivers drain off the hyperarousal in the child's emotional brain and get the young person to a place where he can begin to engage his thinking brain. The 9 skills of becoming a better listener help build the parent–child relationship by making kids feel heard, understood, and valued.

When your child seems to be ready to talk about what happened and language begins to flow, you will know you are ready to move on to the next step of the LSCI approach: *the Timeline*.

CHAPTER 3

BUILDING A TIMELINE
Putting Language to Emotion

In LSCI, the value of careful listening is central to the belief that young people under stress need to talk. As noted in Chapter 2, *how* we listen to kids is critical. As parents and caregivers, we're always trying to link emotions to words. When we help young people put words to their feelings, we empower them to regain control of their emotions and begin to make logical sense of a problem situation.

The objective of listening is to gather enough information about the child's perspective that you can put yourself in his psychological shoes. Listening skills have to do with getting the story from the child's point of view while gathering specific information about the perceptions, thoughts, and feelings that drove troubling behaviors. This is what *building a Timeline* is all about.

In stressful situations, kids do not always recall or relate events factually. They offer a feeling, a behavior, a thought, or a single part of the story that means the most to them. These fragments of memory, coupled with intense emotions, can be difficult for others to follow. *Adults may even begin to believe that their child is intentionally lying about what happened, when in reality brain science shows us clearly that a child's intense emotions can cloud his memory of events.* The LSCI Timeline provides a tool for parents to listen, understand their child's thoughts, and bring order to chaos as he processes a stressful situation. As parents build a child's recollection of events, the child feels heard and understood, which simultaneously soothes the brain and builds a trusting relationship.

> The LSCI Timeline provides a tool for parents to listen, understand their child's thoughts, and bring order to chaos as he processes a stressful situation.

The Timeline and the Conflict Cycle

The building of a Timeline in the LSCI approach uses a process closely linked to the Conflict Cycle to guide kids in exploring key aspects of a problem situation. It is a back-and-forth conversation in which the adult helps kids systematically and carefully understand their personal experience of a troubling event, including their perceptions, thoughts, feelings, behaviors, and the responses of others.

Helpful questions to build a Timeline of a problem situation include the following:

PERCEPTION OF A STRESSFUL EVENT

- Help me understand…
- What happened?
- Where did it happen?
- When did it happen?
- Who was involved?
- How long did it go on?
- How often does it happen?
- Who else was involved?

CHILD'S THOUGHTS

- What went through your mind when that happened?
- Do you remember what you were thinking at that point?
- What were you saying to yourself when that occurred?

CHILD'S FEELINGS

- How did that make you feel?
- On a scale of 1 to 10, how angry/sad/frustrated/etc. were you?
- Do you remember how you were feeling when he said that?

CHILD'S BEHAVIORS

- What did you do when you were feeling so angry/sad/frustrated/etc.?
- How did you show your feelings?
- On a scale of 1 to 10, how hard did you hit … loud did you yell … etc.?

OTHERS' REACTIONS

- What did your sister do when you yelled at her?
- How did Dad react when you said that?
- Then what happened?
- Did things seem to get better or worse for you after that?

Tips for Building an Effective Timeline

As the parent or caregiver gathers information about the problem situation from the young person's point of view, he is careful to:

- ASK questions that prompt a child's orderly recollection of details, while at the same time…

- AVOID making the child feel like he is being interrogated.

> The goal of building a Timeline is to help a young person put language to emotion and begin to make sense of a problem situation.

Questions to Ask to Obtain a Good Timeline

PERCEPTIONS AND IRRATIONAL BELIEFS

Incident
Help me understand...
What happened?
Where did it happen?
When did it happen?
Who was involved?
How long did it go on?
How tough was it?
How often does it happen?
Were others involved?
(Look for patterns.)

Thoughts
- What went through your mind?
- You must have had some thoughts about that.
- What were you saying to yourself at this point?

Feelings
How did that make you feel?
On a scale of 1 to 10, how angry...sad...disappointed... etc., were you?
(Determine intensity.)

Behavior
What did you do when you were feeling...(so upset)?

How did you show your feelings?

On a scale of 1 to 10, how hard did you hit...loud did you yell...etc.

Others' Reactions
How did the teacher... other student(s)... guard...etc...respond?

Then what happened?

The goal of building a Timeline is never about "making the child admit what he did" or "catching him in a lie" but rather is always grounded in helping a young person put language to emotion and begin to make sense of a problem situation. This involves the adult prompting a child with detail-oriented questions while still using the core skills of Drain Off (see Chapter 2) to talk in supportive, relationship-building ways.

During the process of building a Timeline, the parent or caregiver should offer affirming comments while also checking for understanding. In an effective Timeline, the adult takes the opportunity to rephrase what the young person says:

- You are handling a difficult situation really well. I'm impressed. You told me that when you were telling the story at dinner and Grace laughed out loud, you thought she was making fun of you. That's when you said… Do I have that right so far?

You will also want to summarize as the story goes on. As you do this, you're bringing order to chaos. You are creating a clearer sequence of events. Often, when a child is under stress, he can't give you a nice, logical, sequential order of exactly what happened. He has many thoughts, feelings, and memories, but they are often out of order. By summarizing and reflecting on it with the child, you can bring order to all of that emotion.

- Wow. You just told me a lot of information! Thank you for being so detailed. I'm really starting to understand why this situation was so stressful or you. Is it OK if I just say some of this back to you so I can make sure I am remembering everything? So, you were walking home from the park with Shea when she told you that you weren't going to make the basketball team. That's when you started to feel… You told Shea that… Then Shea said… By the time you got home, you were already feeling… When I asked you to start your homework, you…

The tone of a Timeline conversation should be mutual problem solving . The parent and child are putting their heads together to try to figure out what went wrong. Don't get bogged down in trying to get the wording of your questions exactly right or trying to ask every single one of the questions we offer as a sample. Kids don't care nearly as much about *what* you say as they care that you are genuinely interested

> The tone of a Timeline conversation should be *mutual problem solving*.

in their thoughts and feelings. Their radar is usually precise. Adults going through the motions of a Timeline and asking rote questions will be mistrusted on the spot. On the other hand, parents who give of their time, listen well, show interest, and take kids seriously are usually deemed trustworthy.

Building a helpful Timeline is likened to asking the young person to replay in his mind a movie of the event. The parent helps the child examine the events "scene by scene," focusing in on certain features and providing a wide-angle view of others. In this way, several things are accomplished.

1. The parent seeks to understand the child's point of view. This willingness to see things from the child's psychological world builds trust and breaks down the child's defensiveness.

2. The parent gains insight into the underlying causes of his child's behavior. Rather than focusing solely on poor, impulsive behavior, the parent now understands how events occurred from the child's point of view as well as from the point of view of other adults, siblings, or peers involved.

3. The parent helps the child create a new understanding by asking a series of questions that cast the events in a new perspective.

Putting LSCI Skills Together: A Drain-Off and Timeline Example

One thing that we have working for us in LSCI is that most kids really want to tell their story. They just don't want to be interrupted, contradicted, ridiculed, or humiliated. They want to confide in somebody they can trust. The process of LSCI makes it easier for kids to develop trust in parents and caregivers because of the way the adults encourage children to tell their story.

In the section below, you will read an example of a mother using the LSCI skills of Drain Off and Timeline with her son, Tommy. As you read, consider how the mother helped soothe Tommy's intense feelings and supported him to tell his story. Make note of specific questions and phrases you find most effective in draining off Tommy's emotions and helping him put words to his feelings.

Background Information

Ten-year-old Tommy got up in the morning and started to get ready for school. Usually, he gets ready independently, but this day, he was having difficulty. He took longer in the bathroom than usual. He complained loudly of not having the right cereal at breakfast, and he argued with his sister about whose job it was to feed the cat.

When it came time to leave for the bus, Tommy couldn't find his shoes. He began throwing things around the house. He picked up the remote control and threw it across the room saying, "I'm sick and tired of people trying to control my life."

Step 1: Drain Off

Mother:	Whoa, Tommy. You are not acting like yourself at all this morning Are you OK?
Tommy:	(Throws a pillow at the ground.) I'm fine! I'm just sick and tired of everyone trying to control me! That's all!
Mother:	OK. I hear you. You are feeling angry right now because you think that people are trying to control you. Is that right?
Tommy:	(Sits down.) Yes! I hate it!
Mother:	I can understand that, Tommy. It's frustrating when other people seem to be telling you what to do all of the time. Did something happen this morning?
Tommy:	No one is telling me what to do! You're not even listening to me!

Mother: I know you are trying to help me understand what's going on. Sometimes I get it wrong on the first try. Would you like a drink of water?

Tommy: No! I'm going to miss my bus. I can't even find my shoes. And now I broke the remote, and I know I'm going to have to fix it. This is going to be the worst day ever.

Mother: (In a soothing but authoritative voice) Tommy, it's almost impossible to think straight when you have so many worries going on in your head all at once. Let me take one worry off of your plate right now. I am going to drive you to school today. I don't want you to have to worry about rushing, and you don't need to panic about your shoes. Let's just take a minute to have a drink of water and catch our breath. I think we could both use that right now, OK?

Tommy: OK. But what about the remote?

Mother: We can talk about the remote later. At this moment, the most important thing to me is you and helping you feel better so that we can figure this out together.

Tommy: So, you're not mad at me about the remote?

Mother: (Brings over a glass of water for each of them and sits down next to Tommy on the sofa.) I'm not mad at you about the remote.

Tommy and his mother sit together for about 30 seconds in a calm silence, drinking their water and just breathing. Tommy's mother hands him a soft foam ball that is sitting on a nearby table. She encourages him to squeeze the ball as she begins to talk again.

Mother: Thank you for being willing to sit here with me quietly, Tommy. Let's see if we can figure this out together.

Tommy: It's just a terrible week, and everything is going wrong.

Mother: You feel like everything is going wrong this week. Throwing the remote was your way of showing me how upset you are feeling. It's OK to just tell me this in words next time.

Tommy: I know, but you are going to be really mad if I tell you!

Mother: Are you still worried about the remote?

Tommy: No. It's something else.

Mother: I want to help you with whatever it is that is making you this upset, Tommy. Even if it is something that makes me feel angry, that's OK. We can be angry at each other sometimes and still love each other. I'll try to help you no matter how I may be feeling.

Tommy: Are you sure? Promise not to be mad?

Mother: I promise that even if I am mad, I will still love you just the same amount and will still try to help you. Is that fair?

Tommy: OK.

Step 2: Timeline

Mother: Good. OK. So you said before that it has been a terrible week. I hadn't noticed you feeling upset until this morning. Is it because we ran out of your cereal?

Tommy: No.

Mother: Is it because of something else that happened this morning?

Tommy:	Not really. I just didn't get much sleep.
Mother:	You didn't get much sleep last night? Do you know why?
Tommy:	I was just up thinking all night. (Pauses.) And I was kind of mad at you.
Mother:	You had a lot on your mind last night and were thinking angry thoughts that made it hard for you to sleep.
Tommy:	(Quietly) Yes.
Mother:	Can you tell me what those angry thoughts were about?
Tommy:	(Hesitates for a moment, then seems to start getting worked up again.) I miss seeing Dad, and now that you and him are in another fight, I probably won't be able to go to his house this weekend. That's not fair!
Mother:	(Sensing Tommy's re-escalated mood, uses Reassuring skills.) You know, Tommy, I'll bet it took a lot of courage for you to tell me that. Thank you for trusting me with your thoughts. That was a lot to keep bottled up inside you, and I'm glad you got it out. I'm also proud of you for being so honest with me.
Tommy:	(Looks at his mother, surprised but also emboldened.) And I'm also mad because I think you and Dad fight about stupid things! Like you're mad at him now because he won't send you money to pay for my sports stuff, and he's mad at you because he says you spent too much on my cleats. And I'm the one who's gonna' end up losing out. I hate it!
Mother:	You know what, Tommy? You are right. Dad and I do fight about stupid things sometimes. I am truly sorry for the ways our disagreements affect you.

Tommy:	(Mutters.) It's OK.
Mother:	Dad and I fight about stupid things a lot of the time, but this fight seems to have you extra upset. Can we talk more about what has you feeling so badly?
Tommy:	I guess.
Mother:	Thank you. So, last night Dad and I were talking on the phone about your new uniform, and you must have heard us arguing about money. Is that right?
Tommy:	Yes.
Mother:	Could you hear Dad's part of the conversation too or just mine?
Tommy:	Just your words, but I could hear that Dad was yelling. It stressed me out.
Mother:	I can understand why you felt stressed. I think I was feeling pretty stressed out too. Do you remember what you were thinking while Dad and I were talking?
Tommy:	I was thinking that I wasn't going to get to visit him this weekend. And it made me really mad because we were going to go fishing, and we haven't done that in forever!
Mother:	So, in your head, you were saying to yourself that you were probably going to lose out on your weekend time and fun plans with Dad.
Tommy:	Yes! And it made me really mad, but I didn't want to say anything to you because I didn't want to make you upset, so I just went to bed. But then I couldn't sleep because all night long I was just thinking over and over about how much I miss Dad when I don't get to see him.

Mother: You really love your dad, and you love spending time with him. You know what, Tommy? I really love that about you. I'm happy you love both of your parents.

Tommy: But I always worry that you are going to be mad if I want to visit Dad.

Mother: It's a horrible thing to feel torn between two people that you love. I'm so sorry that you have been feeling that way, but I am also really glad that you told me so that now I can do something about it. I'm getting a better understanding of why you were so stressed out this morning. Since you overheard part of our conversation last night, you have been feeling so angry and worried that you couldn't get much sleep. You didn't want to talk to me about your feelings because you were worried I would be angry, but I'm thinking that it was too hard to hide all of those big feelings, and they started to seep out at your sister and then on the remote. Do you think that might be true?

Tommy: I guess a little.

Mother: Is there anything else that I am forgetting or anything else that you have been upset about?

Tommy: Not really. Just the stuff about Dad and not getting to visit him has me really upset.

Mother: OK. Thank you for being so open about your feelings this morning. I have a few thoughts about everything that I'd like to run by you.

END OF TIMELINE

If you dislike a cliffhanger ending, never fear. The LSCI conversation between Tommy and his mother will be resolved in Chapter 4 as we present all four steps of an LSCI conversation between a parent and a child. In the meantime, let's reflect briefly on what happened during the first two steps (Drain Off and Timeline) of their discussion.

- We give Tommy's mom a lot of credit in this situation. It would have been all too easy for her to allow her emotional brain to take control as she witnessed her son complain about breakfast, argue with his sister, and then throw the remote control across the room. Because she made the choice to look beyond Tommy's destructive behavior and recognize that *nothing comes from nothing*, she was able to stay in her thinking brain and initiate Drain-Off skills to de-escalate the intensity of the situation. As Tommy feels her support, he begins to calm down.

- Tommy was angry and accusatory at the beginning of the situation. (*I'm just sick and tired of everyone trying to control me. You're not even listening to me! This is going to be the worst day ever.*) Note that the mother resists the temptation to react defensively to any of these baiting statements. She skillfully avoids Tommy's clearly worded invitation to the conflict by keeping her focus on using Drain-Off skills. Remember: There is always time to address disrespectful behavior. The heat of the moment is not the right time, however. Doing so is almost guaranteed to escalate a conflict just when what really needs to happen is de-escalation.

- Initially, Tommy seems focused on missing the bus. Later, he is preoccupied by thoughts of his mother being angry over the broken remote control. Notice that the mother does not dismiss his concerns. To do so would likely have escalated his anxiety over both concerns. Rather, she acknowledges both issues (*Let me take one worry off of your plate right now. I am going to drive you to school today. I'm not mad at you about the remote.*) and skillfully "puts them on a shelf" to be resolved later. This enables Tommy to put these concerns to rest in his overwhelmed emotional brain so that he can shift his focus and attention to the most important issues at hand.

- Notice that as the mother is steady in her emotions and consistent in giving support, Tommy begins to talk. After his mother asks what happened to make him feel so upset, he drops a hint about not having slept well. As the mother attends to this piece of information, responds with empathy, and begins to decode the true meaning behind his outburst, Tommy tells her more and more of his story.

- One of the most tempting aspects of the Timeline step in an LSCI conversation is to begin problem solving too soon. Tommy's mother was likely eager to respond with logic or reason to some of Tommy's comments. For example, when he said *"I was thinking that I wasn't going to get to visit him this weekend. And it made me really mad because we were going to go fishing, and we haven't done that in forever!"* his mother may have wanted to say something along the lines of *"Just because Dad and I argue doesn't mean you will lose your visit. You're not a mind reader. You shouldn't jump to conclusions."* Doing so might even have been justified, but it would have sounded defensive to Tommy and would almost certainly have shut down the conversation prematurely. It is critical to remember that the Timeline step is reserved for gathering information about the young person's thoughts, feelings, and behaviors. Problem solving will happen soon—but doing so too early runs the risk of cutting short the conversation and missing important information about the child's point of view.

- Lastly, keep in mind that during a problem situation, allowing a young person to talk about the story from his point of view is essential. Even if you were right there and saw everything that happened, there is great value in getting an understanding of the child's perception, thoughts, and feelings about the events.

FROM TIMELINE TO UNDERSTANDING THE PROBLEM AND SKILL BUILDING

Establishing a good Timeline is a skill that comes with practice. Drain-Off and Timeline skills can be used across any stressful or crisis situation with a young person. Both skills lead to better trust between the parent and child and open up a new understanding of the child's psychological world. The first two steps of the LSCI 4-step process provide an invaluable opportunity for a young person to learn to put words to emotions and gain more control over the feelings and impulses that drive poor behaviors. The Timeline step also opens the door to discussions about the child's choices during a conflict.

In the next chapter, we will show you how the steps for helping a child develop a new understanding of a problem and build new skills to handle problem situations are effectively carried out. We will also show you how the situation between Tommy and his mother is resolved.

CHAPTER 4

THE 4-STEP PROCESS:
Drain Off, Timeline, Understanding the Problem, and Skill Building

LSCI is a structured process that offers parents and caregivers a consistent way to talk with a stressed-out child. It matters little if we are new to parenthood or have been caring for young people for decades. There are times when all kids say or do things that hijack our amygdala and leave us unsure of what to say or do. That's why the LSCI 4-step verbal process is so powerful—it provides a cognitive roadmap that can help keep us in our thinking brains and focused on the goals of helping children calm down, put language to emotion, understand their problem, and learn new skills—even during those inevitable times when our emotional brains really want to take over.

In Chapters 2 and 3, you learned the skills of Drain Off and Timeline, which means you have the knowledge to carry out the first two steps of the 4-step verbal framework. You are already halfway there! The remaining two steps, detailed in this chapter, will guide you in helping kids understand their problems and develop the skills needed to prevent the problems from occurring over and over again.

> LSCI is a structured process that offers parents and caregivers a consistent way to talk with a stressed-out child.

The four steps of LSCI are summarized in the graphic below.

The LSCI 4-Step Verbal Process

Step 1: Drain Off
Attending, reassuring, affirming, validating, and decoding skills to drain off the young person's intense feelings and ready the child for conversation

Step 2: Timeline
Helping the child put language to emotions and gathering specific information about the perceptions, thoughts, and feelings that drove the young person's troubling behaviors

Step 3: Understanding the Problem
Guiding the child to better understand a problem situation and begin to recognize self-defeating behaviors

Step 4: Skill Building
Teaching the young person specific social, emotional, and behavioral skills to change self-defeating behaviors

Before we fully describe Steps 3 and 4, it is important to note that real life is not always laid out in four nice, neat boxed steps, as in the diagram above. In actual conversations with stressed-out young people, the steps flow into each other fluidly, and there can be some back and forth between steps. For example, a child's emotions may have been thoroughly drained off in Step 1, but as she gains a new understanding of her situation in Step 3, she may become agitated again and need additional Drain Off. The 4-step LSCI process offers a great deal of flexibility that allows parents and caregivers to go back and forth between steps during a dialog with a child while still functioning as a clear overall roadmap that guides us to an ultimate goal in each conversation.

Step 3: Understanding the Problem

The third step of the LSCI process involves using the information gathered during Drain Off and Timeline to guide a young person to a new, different, or clearer understanding of a problem situation. In Step 3, the parent or caregiver continues to use supportive statements and focused questions to help the child make sense of a stressful event as independently and spontaneously as possible.

To be effective in carrying out this stage of the LSCI approach, adults must avoid using Step 3 as a time to lecture kids on where they went wrong, spoon feed their own perceptions about a problem, assign rote punishments, or indulge in an *"I've told you this a million times already"* reminder. Rather, Step 3 works best when adults continue to affirm and validate a child's psychological world while simultaneously offering more helpful ways of perceiving, thinking, feeling, or responding to a stressful situation.

The process of Step 3 can be compared to a video camera and its operator. As the young person is telling his story during the Timeline step, he is showing us a video of how he saw the situation. Our job during the Timeline is to see that videotape clearly. As we view it, we'll find things that are missing—places where the camera was focused on only one small aspect of the event or places where the view was so wide that it missed essential details.

The supportive statements and focused questions we ask during Step 3 of the LSCI process focus in on those missing pieces where the camera had a blocked or blurry view. As parents and caregivers, our task is to reframe the footage of the event in order to help the video make better sense. As you work together through Step 3, your child will gain a new understanding of a stressful event and begin to recognize how his behavior contributed to it.

Step 4: Skill Building

For us natural teachers and problem solvers, here is the step you have been waiting for! Step 4 in the LSCI approach is a time for building the social, emotional, and/or behavioral skills a young person needs to respond more constructively to a stressful event or problem situation.

When carried through effectively, a child emerges from Step 3 with a new understanding of a problem and a recognition of how his behavior contributed to the situation. Knowing *what went wrong* is a critical milestone in the problem-solving process, yet it is virtually worthless if not paired with teaching a young person the skills she needs to make things right moving forward . This is the goal of Step 4.

> Knowing *what went wrong* is a critical milestone in the problem-solving process.

A hallmark of LSCI is its back-and-forth, empowering dialog, which means that Step 4 should remain an exchange of ideas between the adult and child rather than an authoritarian *"I'm going to tell you how to fix this"* time period. In Step 4, the parent or caregiver asks questions and uses supportive statements to guide the young person in exploring what he could have done differently and what skills he needs to make a better behavioral choice next time. Further, young people *learn by doing;* therefore, role playing and practicing new skills is a great way for parents to support their child's ability to carry out the new skills learned in LSCI.

Below, we explore three of the most essential skills kids need to constructively manage stressful situations.

1. Self-Regulation

Knowing that so many of a young person's poor behaviors are linked to impulsive, amygdala-driven emotional responses to stressful events, *self-regulation* is a critical skill to build in almost all young people. Self-regulation is the ability to control emotions and resist impulsive behaviors. Children who have good emotional self-regulation have the ability to keep their emotions in check. They can resist impulsive behaviors that might worsen their situation, and they can cheer themselves up when they're feeling down. What's more, children with strong self-regulation skills possess a range of emotional and behavioral responses that are well matched to the demands of their situation (Bell, 2016).

> Self-regulation is the ability to control emotions and resist impulsive behaviors.

Although a comprehensive discussion of how to cultivate self-regulation skills in young people is beyond the scope of this book, a few key considerations include:

- For some young people, self-regulation seems to come as naturally as breathing. For others, learning to control emotions and resist impulses is a process that develops over time and through lots (and lots!) of practice. Don't feel badly about yourself or your child if she needs more time than others to develop self-regulation skills. Simply give her what she needs—time, space, and a supportive environment—to develop these critical skills.

- Even young children can benefit from understanding that they have both an emotional part of their brain and a thinking part of their brain. Daniel Siegel's Hand-Brain Model is a great resource for breaking down complex brain functions into simple terms kids can understand. A brief video by Siegel is available on YouTube at https://www.youtube.com/watch?v=gm9CIJ74Oxw&t=6s.

- Mindfulness practices are a fantastic way of helping kids develop the skill of controlling their emotional responses and resisting the impulsive behaviors that tend to get them in trouble.

- Approach the teaching of self-regulation skills in the same way as you would teach your child any other skill he needs to succeed—by providing practice and affording patience. Just as you would not expect your child to know how to ride a bicycle simply by discussing the mechanics of pedaling, parents and caregivers should not expect that learning to control emotions and resist impulses will happen through one LSCI conversation. Rather, know with certainty that self-regulation skills will need to be practiced over and over again.

- Do not make the mistake of avoiding tough situations just because your child may struggle with them. This approach leaves kids feeling powerless. Instead, be there for your child to coach her through stressful events. Anticipate when problem situations are likely to occur, plan for how to handle them, coach your child in the moment to stay calm and resist impulses, and then offer praise and constructive feedback after the fact.

2. Social Skills

Social skills is an umbrella term for the ability to get along with others and adjust our behavior to fit a particular situation (Kennedy-Moore, 2011). Like self-regulation, social skills come naturally to some young people and are an ever-present struggle for others. No matter where your child falls on the social skills spectrum, know that as a parent or caregiver, you have the opportunity to guide him in his socialization and give him the practical experience he needs to improve.

Typical social skills that can be discussed, developed, and practiced through the LSCI process include:

- Expressing feelings in constructive ways
- Problem solving, compromise, and conflict resolution
- Speaking in a respectful tone and using appropriate volume
- Using good eye contact
- Making and refusing requests
- Empathy and compassion for others
- Getting along with siblings
- Understanding cause and effect
- Being flexible; handling changes in plans
- Friendship skills (e.g., how to make a friend, how to handle teasing, how to handle rejection)

3. Good Decision Making

Step 4 is a time for brainstorming solution strategies with your child. Often, kids come up with very wise, intuitive problem-solving ideas once their emotional brain is soothed and they have had the experience of being heard, understood, and valued. Still, there are times late in an LSCI conversation when a young person's frustration still rises to the surface and you may hear him suggest an unwise solution for handling a problem. That's OK. It's even predictable. As parents and caregivers, we are wise to not reject kids' solutions right away but rather to help nurture their good decision making instead. That means that we guide our kids through the skill of calmly considering the possible outcomes of any behavioral choice and walk them through the various possibilities until we reach a mutually acceptable decision. Ultimately, we'll teach and rehearse the skills needed for success.

STEPS 3 AND 4 IN PRACTICE

In the pages that follow, we revisit the dialog between Tommy and his mother that we began in Chapter 3. We pick up at the end of the Timeline step and show you how the mom used Steps 3 and 4 of the LSCI process to guide her son to a successful resolution to their conflict.

> ## The Situation
>
> Ten-year-old Tommy got up in the morning and started to get ready for school. Usually, he gets ready independently, but this day, he was having difficulty. He took longer in the bathroom than usual. He complained loudly of not having the right cereal at breakfast, and he argued with his sister about whose job it was to feed the cat.
>
> When it came time to leave for the bus, Tom couldn't find his shoes. He began throwing things around the house. He picked up the remote control and threw it across the room saying, "I'm sick and tired of people trying to control my life."

(Picking up at the very end of the Timeline step)

Mother: Is there anything else that I am forgetting or anything else that you have been upset about?

Tommy: Not really. Just the stuff about Dad and not getting to visit him has me really upset.

Mother: OK. Thank you for being so open about your feelings this morning. I have a few thoughts about everything that I'd like to run by you.

Step 3: Understanding the Problem

Mother: Earlier, you told me that you started feeling angry last night when you overheard Dad and I talking on the phone, right?

Tommy: Right.

Mother: You told me that you heard the things I was saying, and even though you couldn't hear Dad's exact words, you could tell he was yelling. The whole thing stressed you out.

Tommy: Exactly.

Mother: The thing that I am confused about is what made you think that you were not going to be able to go to Dad's this weekend. Did you think you heard me say that?

Tommy: Well, no, but I just figured it would probably happen. Every time something bad happens with you and Dad, it feels like I am the one who suffers.

Mother: You feel like bad things happen to you when Dad and I fight.

Tommy: It just seems like you and Dad are used to fighting, and it doesn't even bother you, but I am the one who gets upset, and then I usually end up getting in trouble.

Mother: Wow, Tommy. What you just said is really important.

Tommy: (Looks puzzled.) What do you mean?

Mother: Well, let's be honest. Divorce can be tough on a family. Constant fighting between parents definitely can affect kids. What you are helping me understand is that when you overhear Dad and I arguing—even if it's over "stupid things" that don't really even make us feel upset—you have your own set of thoughts and feelings about our fight. In this case, your feelings were so strong that they caused you to jump to some conclusions about what might happen next. Specifically, you assumed you would not get to go to Dad's house this weekend, and you would miss out on going fishing with him.

Tommy: Well, yeah. Is that what's going to happen? Do we have to cancel the visit?

Mother: We have absolutely no plans to cancel your visit to Dad's this weekend, Tommy. Your dad and I did bicker about money last night. You heard that exactly correctly. But as you said just a minute ago, we did not talk at all about plans for the weekend. Is it possible that your feelings about us fighting took over your thinking and caused you to assume your weekend plans would be ruined?

Tommy: I guess.

Mother: There is something else you said a minute ago that I thought was really important. You said that when you get upset, you usually end up getting in trouble. I am wondering if your angry thoughts and feelings cause you to act out in ways that get you in trouble and maybe even cause exactly the kind of consequence that you were worried about in the first place.

Tommy: I'm not totally sure I am following that last part.

Mother: Let me ask you this: Do you think your angry thoughts and feelings that were brewing last night are what caused you to yell at your sister and throw the remote this morning?

Tommy: Probably.

Mother: After you did those things, your upset mind jumped to the conclusion that you were going to be punished. You assumed I would tell you that you couldn't visit Dad this weekend—which is exactly what you spent last night worrying might happen. In other words, your behaviors could have resulted in your worries coming true. Does that make more sense?

Tommy: Yeah, it makes sense. I think maybe that kind of thing happens to me a lot. I get upset about something I think is going to happen, and even though I try really hard to hold my feelings in so that I don't get you or Dad upset, I usually end up exploding and getting myself into trouble.

Mother: I think you have realized a pattern that does seem to happen a lot to you, Tommy. The good thing is that knowledge is power, and now that you have this new understanding, I can help you come up with different ways to handle your feelings when you get upset.

Step 4: Skill Building

Tommy: That would be good, I guess.

Mother: Great. Well, for starters, I'm thinking that trying to hide all of your upset feelings is not a helpful choice for you. It puts a lot of pressure on you and ends up resulting in you doing things that get you in trouble. What do you think you could do instead of trying to hide your feelings?

Tommy: I don't know.

Mother: Would you consider telling me when you are upset using your words instead of throwing things like the remote?

Tommy: I don't want to tell you because I don't want you to get upset.

Mother: OK, Tommy. I definitely understand that sometimes the person with whom you are upset can be the hardest person to talk to about your feelings. I would never insist that you have to talk to me when you are angry. Maybe we should try to think about someone else you could talk to when you are upset or find a different way you can deal with your angry feelings so that you don't explode. But first, I do want to point out to you that today,

	you did tell me about your angry feelings, and I think we are having a pretty helpful conversation about them. Instead of being mad at you, I'm actually really proud of you for having the courage to be so honest with me. I can't promise that I'll never get angry with you when you tell me things. Sometimes my emotions take over just like yours do. I admit it. But I can promise you that I am learning from this conversation just like you are, and I will do my best to stay calm and be open to you anytime you want to tell me about your feelings. OK?
Tommy:	OK. That would be nice.
Mother:	In the event that you still feel like you can't tell me something or I am not around when you are feeling upset, let's think about someone else you could talk to or something else you could do.
Tommy:	Well, I don't really like talking to kids my own age about stuff like this, but listening to music usually helps me feel better. And playing soccer definitely gets my mind off of bad things—but I can't go outside and play soccer in the dark if I hear you and Dad fighting at night.
Mother:	No. Playing soccer at night outside in the dark is probably not going to work, but kicking the ball around during the day is a fantastic way to deal with stress. For stress that you feel at night, either listening to some music or talking to someone else are good ideas. Do you think you could talk to your sister? She's probably a good person for understanding how you feel.
Tommy:	Maybe. But we always end up taking our moods out on each other. I think I'd rather just read or play a video game or do something else to distract myself for a while. When I'm not as mad, I will try to talk to you.
Mother:	I think that sounds like a perfect plan, Tommy. I will also try to help remind you to use those strategies if I notice you are getting upset. Having a drink of water and taking some deep breaths seemed to help you today too.

Tommy: Yeah. Sort of.

Mother: "Sort of" is a start. Is there anything else that is on your mind that we didn't talk about yet?

Tommy: No. Not really. I think I need to get to school before it gets any later.

Mother: OK. Can we check in after school again for just a few minutes to make sure we're all good and that there's nothing else we need to clear the air about? Maybe that's also a good time to check out the remote and see if we need to fix it.

Tommy: Sure. I'll fix it if anything's broken. I know how to take it apart.

Mother: Sounds like a good plan.

REVIEW OF STEPS 3 AND 4

This situation between Tommy and his mother started off with what appeared to be an angry, explosive young man taking out his feelings on anyone and everyone around him. In many households, this kind of disrespectful, aggressive behavior would have sparked an equally angry, perhaps punitive or hurtful response, from an adult and ultimately resulted in a damaged relationship between the parent and child.

The skills of LSCI allowed Tommy's mother to bring about a different, better outcome. After her effective use of Drain-Off and Timeline skills (see Chapter 3), the mother used the information from these first two steps of the LSCI process to help Tommy begin to understand his problem in a new way.

One of the mother's most effective tools in Step 3 is her careful use of key phrases and supportive questions. For example, rather than telling Tommy straightaway that he must have misheard her call with his dad or berating him for jumping to the wrong conclusion, the mother guides her son to come to this insight on his own:

- *The thing that I am confused about is what made you think that you were not going to be able to go to Dad's this weekend. Did you think you heard me say that?*

- *Is it possible that your feelings about us fighting took over your thinking and caused you to assume your weekend plans would be ruined?*

Likewise, in helping Tommy understand the role his own behaviors played in the problem situation, the mother effectively "wonders" aloud:

- *I am wondering if your angry thoughts and feelings cause you to act out in ways that get you in trouble—and maybe even cause exactly the kind of consequence that you were worried about in the first place.*

One of Tommy's chief concerns throughout the conversation is his assumption that he might not get to visit his dad. In the section below, note how the mother recognizes his preoccupation and addresses it simply and straightforwardly so that it does not become a roadblock to deeper conversation:

Tommy: Is that what's going to happen? Do we have to cancel the visit?

Mother: We have absolutely no plans to cancel your visit to Dad's this weekend, Tommy.

With this vital concern addressed directly, she went on to affirm Tommy's belief that she and his father were arguing the night before. In this way, she modeled honesty, thereby opening the door wider for Tommy to trust her:

Mother: Your dad and I did bicker about money last night. You heard that exactly correctly. But as you said just a minute ago, we did not talk at all about plans for the weekend. Is it possible that your feelings about us fighting took over your thinking and caused you to assume your weekend plans would be ruined?

After achieving the goal of Step 3 by helping Tommy understand how his emotions drove his aggressive behaviors, the mother used Step 4 to focus on building self-regulation skills. She offered her support in discussing with Tommy different ways to handle his feelings when he gets upset. Note her phrasing as she empowered him to identify options independently and also worked with him to generate helpful ideas:

- *What do you think you could do instead of trying to hide your feelings?*
- *Would you consider telling me when you are upset—using your words instead of throwing things like the remote?*
- *Maybe we should try to think about someone else you could talk to when you are upset or find a different way you can deal with your angry feelings so that you don't explode.*
- *Do you think you could talk to your sister?*
- *Having a drink of water and taking some deep breaths seemed to help you today too.*

The mother helped Tommy weigh his different options and decide on things such as the right time of day for each option and different people in whom he can confide.

Lastly, at the end of the conversation, the mother returned to the issue of the remote control. Some parents and caregivers may believe that dealing with the damaged property is the primary issue in this conflict. Tommy certainly did early on. Others who view problem situations as learning opportunities might see a damaged remote control as a small price to pay for a young man to come to understand that he has a pattern of jumping to conclusions during stressful situations and acting out in ways that are self-defeating. In this light, learning new self-regulation skills to manage anger would be seen as an end that justified the means.

No matter your perspective, we can probably all agree that teaching kids to respect property and practice safe behaviors is a worthy goal and that Tommy's mother made sure to close the loop on this lingering issue. The beauty and usefulness of the LSCI process is in its flexibility to manage multiple aspects of a problem situation. Its orderly framework ensures that important issues can be addressed in due time.

PART 2: THE SIX INTERVENTIONS

You have now reached the end of Part 1 of *Parenting the Challenging Child*. You have learned the three foundations of LSCI and gained knowledge of the 4-step LSCI process.

In Part 2 of this book, you will learn about six of the most common patterns of problem behavior among young people and how to apply the consistent 4-step process to each type of stressful situation. Each chapter begins with a real-life problem situation involving a parent and child(ren) and provides step-by-step commentary and guidance on how to use the 4-step process to create lasting changes in the young person's perceptions, thoughts, feelings, and behaviors. You will learn versatile and valuable strategies to use with children who do the following:

1. Act out in stress, sparking explosive and endless power struggles.
2. Make poor decisions based on distorted perceptions and thoughts.
3. Have the right intentions but lack the social skills to be successful.
4. Are purposefully aggressive with little conscience.
5. Act in impulsive ways due to feelings of shame and inadequacy.
6. Become entangled in destructive sibling and peer relationships.

CHAPTER 5

THE SOS INTERVENTION
Identifying the Real Source of the Stress

Ray is a 9-year-old boy who is small for his age and intimidated by older, bigger kids. On the school bus, a teenager named Nate repeatedly threatens Ray and humiliates him in front of the other kids. One afternoon, Nate took the math homework Ray had just completed, tore it into shreds, and threw it out of the bus window. Ray felt helpless. He didn't know how he could keep his property safe around Nate. On top of that, he was furious that none of his friends stepped in to help. Ray arrived home feeling defeated, embarrassed, and angry. When his father asked him to get started on his homework, Ray refused to open his backpack, swore at his dad, kicked the kitchen table, and yelled, "Why won't you just leave me alone already?"

To Ray's father, this response seemed to come completely out of the blue. "All I did," the father insisted to his wife later that evening, "*was ask Ray to start his homework—same as I do every other day when he gets home. You would have thought I asked him to scrub the floors with a toothbrush with that reaction!*"

Indeed, it happens more often than any parent would like that a seemingly minor or routine request is met with a major emotional response or meltdown. As brain science explains, it is natural for adults who are on the receiving end of a child's rage to react with anger of their own (see Chapter 1); however, it is just as certain that "catching" the young person's anger, as if it were a contagious disease, only worsens the situation and damages the parent–child relationship.

Instead of mirroring your child's anger and escalating the problem, bear in mind that *nothing comes from nothing.* This four-word mantra, followed by its three-word counterpart, *look beyond behavior,* is a powerful and effective reminder to parents and caregivers everywhere that a child's surface behavior (e.g., swearing, kicking, yelling) is not always directly related to an immediate stress (e.g., a request to start homework) but rather may be due to other experiences and unresolved feelings (e.g., Ray's mistreatment at the hands of Nate).

Whenever a young person's reaction seems out of proportion to the situation at hand, LSCI guides parents and caregivers to recognize the very real possibility that there's more to the situation than meets the eye. To avoid responding in a way that will make the situation worse instead of better, adults should:

1. First and foremost, remain calm.

This sounds easy enough, but in practice, it can be challenging for even the most easygoing adults to keep their cool when they are on the receiving end of a young person's anger.

Nevertheless, angry and aggressive responses from adults only escalate the child's amygdala-based response and intensify the problem situation. Effective parents and caregivers know that their calm, soothing presence is the best way to help their child regain their composure and begin to deal with the problem in a logical, constructive way.

2. Seek to identify the real source of stress (SOS).

Once the young person's emotional response has been thoroughly drained off and he is back to a place where he can use the logical, rational part of his brain, your next priority is to use Timeline skills (See Chapter 3) to assist him in understanding the true source of his distress. Timeline skills are the key to helping young people put words to their emotions and identify who or what is really bothering them.

Who is in charge in this family ?

If you are a parent or caregiver who wonders, "How will my child ever respect my authority if I don't use my anger to show him who is in charge?" you are not alone. Yet when we allow ourselves to be driven by the emotional part of our brain, we come to mistakenly believe that anger and force are the only ways to establish control over challenging people and situations. *In reality, the ability to remain calm and maintain composure in stressful situations is the very best sign of control that exists.* Know this: A parent's steadiness can bring about increased calm in their kids as well. This phenomena, called *co-regulation* (McKnight, 2016), is exactly the type of real control that is needed to effectively deal with a difficult situation.

What about punishment for misbehavior?

Likewise, you are not alone if your instinct is to use punishment to address surface behaviors in the heat of the moment. Unfortunately, this instinct is counterproductive because it often retriggers the young person's emotional state and typically ends a conversation before the heart of the matter (the actual source of the stress) has been identified. *Kids whose behaviors are met with automatic punishment rather than with real understanding are kids who are doomed to repeat their misbehaviors over and over again.*

Does that mean kids should get off scot-free when they misbehave?

Of course not. There is a need for parents and caregivers to guide young people to understand that actions have consequences. The reality is, however, that the heat of the moment is never the most effective time for kids to learn about accountability, and most punishments given out in anger are ineffective in addressing the actual behavior or teaching the young person better ways to behave in the future.

The Dynamics of Displacement in an SOS Situation

Displacement is the term used in LSCI training to describe situations in which a person takes his anger out on someone or something other than the actual target of his anger. The displacement of intense, uncomfortable emotions is a common self-defeating behavior among children and adults alike. There are many reasons why people displace anger, including the following:

- They fear retaliation by the actual target.
- They don't have the opportunity to express their feelings to the actual target.
- They feel safer taking their anger out on someone else.

Yet displaced anger can damage the very relationships we need the most.

Ironically, it is because of the love and comfort that parents and caregivers provide that their kids may choose them as the persons on whom to displace the anger they feel toward others. Do parents deserve to have their children's bad moods taken out on them? No. Not at all. Are parents in an excellent position to help their kids learn better ways to deal with anger through the way they choose to respond to their children's displacement? Yes, without a doubt! *The power of the SOS intervention comes in helping kids talk about their feelings rather than acting them out onto undeserving caregivers.*

> The power of the SOS intervention comes in helping kids talk about their feelings rather than acting them out onto underserving caregivers.

The 4-Step Process at Work in an SOS Situation

Parents and caregivers play a vital role in helping their kids express anger and other intense emotions in positive, relationship-building ways. Read on to learn how LSCI's 4-step process can guide you to effectively deal with your child's displacement-fueled problem situation.

Step 1: Use the process of Drain Off to help a child reduce the intensity of his emotions.

- Your first priority is to drain off the intensity of your child's feelings. In order to do so, it is essential that you maintain your own calm and composure.

- Use the attending, reassuring, affirming, validating, and decoding skills described in Chapter 2 to meet a young person's basic need to feel heard, understood, and valued.

- Recognize that *nothing comes from nothing;* whenever a child's anger seems out of proportion to the event or appears to come "out of the blue," your ultimate task is to help the young person identify the real source of his stress.

Step 2: Use the Timeline to help a child put language to his emotions.

- Once the young person's anger is thoroughly drained off, use the Timeline skills detailed in Chapter 3 to help him put his emotions into words and begin to engage the problem-solving part of his brain.

- In order to find out if displaced anger is the cause of the problem, it is beneficial to ask questions that help a child identify the source of his anger. In an SOS situation, encourage the young person to think about who he is really mad at versus who received his anger.

- You will know you are ready to move on to Step 3 of the process when the child's emotional state remains calm; he has been able to use words to describe his perceptions, thoughts, and feelings about what happened; and you have a clear understanding of the events that have taken place.

- o If you do not feel completely clear on the timeline of events or your child still seems to be struggling to make sense out of the situation, continue to ask Timeline questions to gain clarity. Do not be discouraged if it takes awhile to get all of the details or to understand your child's point of view. You are not doing anything wrong! The more intense the emotion of the situation, the longer it often takes to make good sense of it.

- o A helpful way to transition from Step 2 to Step 3 is to summarize the young person's story from beginning to end. In doing so, you show the child that you have truly listened and paid attention to his point of view. What's more, hearing about the problem situation in someone else's words assists the child in gaining needed clarity about the events.

Step 3: Understand the problem—recognize the dynamics of displacement.

- Once the true source(s) of anger has been identified using the Timeline step, it is time to shift your focus from information gathering to helping the child understand the problem in a new way.

- Begin Step 3 by asking the young person questions to help distinguish the source of his anger from the recipient of his anger. In this way, you help your child begin to understand the dynamic of displacement.

- In any situation where anger is being displaced, it is human nature for the undeserving recipient of the anger to react emotionally. To genuinely help children, however, parents and caregivers need to be able to recognize the dynamics of displacement as they are occurring and to make a conscious decision not to engage a child in a no-win power struggle.

In an SOS situation, teaching kids skills to express anger in constructive ways is essential.

Step 4: Teach your child new skills for expressing anger constructively.

- Step 4 is a skill-building stage. Here, rather than punishing a child for the angry, aggressive behaviors you don't like, you have the opportunity to teach him the skills he needs to behave better in the future. In an SOS situation teaching kids skills to express anger in constructive ways is essential.

- At this point, it is helpful to engage your child in a back-and-forth conversation about healthy ways to express anger. You may want to share certain strategies that have worked for you in the past and challenge him to think about what does (and does not) usually work for him.

- Encourage your child to come up with at least one or two anger management ideas of his own, but also feel free to offer skills for healthy anger expression, such as the following:

    o Recognizing the early warning signs of anger in his body (e.g., rapid heart rate, hot face, hands balled into fists, a tightening in the chest)

    o Choosing to take a break from a situation when these early warning signs are first detected

    o Taking 10 deep breaths

    o Using a journal to write about his feelings

    o Talking about feelings of anger with safe people

- Step 4 is completed when both you and your child feel satisfied that the problem situation has been discussed, a new understanding of the dynamic of displacement has emerged, and he feels better equipped with strategies to manage angry, uncomfortable emotions the next time they arise.

Will Using the 4-Step Process Prevent All Future SOS Situations?

Realistically, one SOS intervention is not going to radically change a child's life or ensure that a young person never overreacts to a routine request again. If behaviors were that easy to change, you wouldn't be reading this book in the first place. Managing anger is a challenge to people of most ages, and learning how to do so consistently is a process for all of us. The 4-step process outlined above is an important step in the process of helping kids gain control over their emotions because it offers them three key benefits:

1. The experience of putting their feelings into words and feeling heard, understood, and valued

2. Understanding of the relationship-damaging dynamic of displacement

3. New skills to better manage anger in future situations

Parents and caregivers who use the 4-step process with kids in an SOS situation should not expect to never have to remind them how to express anger effectively. Both in school and in life, young people learn through repetition and practice. Thus, with consistency and opportunities to test out their new skills, they benefit each time the SOS approach is used. Over time, using the SOS intervention reduces the need to reuse the SOS intervention in the future. You'll know that consistency has paid off when your child begins to initiate positive anger management skills during stressful situations and reduces instances of displacement.

> **Young people learn through repetition and practice. When used consistently, kids stand to benefit each time the SOS approach is used.**

> ## When Children Express Anger Appropriately
>
> A final note for parents and caregivers before moving on to an example of how the 4-step process could sound in real life: It is essential that, as your young person develops and begins to use new skills for healthy anger expression, you are willing to accept the anger and affirm its constructive expression.
>
> Adults who take a child's anger personally and become angry, offended, or defensive can unwittingly undo the positive effects of the SOS intervention. Even if your words may say "Let's try to work through this together," if your body language, tone of voice, or actions show that you are angry at your child for feeling angry, he will not feel safe enough to talk about his feelings or learn new skills for managing them.
>
> On the other hand, when parents understand that their child's anger is not a personal insult, they send the message that anger is a natural human response to frustrating conditions and that their relationship with their child can withstand the respectful expression of this basic human emotion.

The 4-Step Process With Ray and His Father

In the pages that follow, we offer you an example of what an SOS intervention between Ray and his father could sound like using the 4-step process. It is important to note that there is no "script" to an LSCI intervention. Your conversation with your child does not have to sound precisely like our example. In fact, authenticity is essential for connecting with kids and bringing about genuine changes in their thoughts, feelings, and behaviors. Therefore, this example is offered as a general guide to provide useful phrases for Drain Off (Step 1), effective Timeline questions (Step 2), helpful ways to understand the dynamic of displacement (Step 3), and practical skills for positive anger management (Step 4).

Step 1: Use the process of Drain Off to help a child reduce the intensity of his emotions.

Ray: (Yelling, pacing around the room, head down) Why won't you just leave me alone already?

Dad: (In a calm, lowered voice) I can see that you are really worked up and upset right now.

Ray: (Silent, looks at father.)

Dad: Let's just sit here together for a few minutes and see if we can work this out. Would you like some cold water to drink?

Ray: (Shakes his head no to the water but sits down at the kitchen table.)

Dad: (Sits at the table with Ray.) Thanks for sitting with me. I know it's hard to come home from a long day at school and then have parents start talking about homework right away. I apologize if I made you feel pressured.

Ray: I don't feel pressured! I'm mad! I hate math! I hate the bus! I hate everyone!

Dad: The fact that you were willing to sit here with me, even when you are feeling so mad and so much hate, shows me that despite it all, you are trying to get back in control and willing to work things out. I'm really impressed. It's not easy to sit and talk when your whole body is filled with anger.

Ray: I've never even done anything to Nate, but he keeps picking on me every single day. And no one does anything about it. The bus driver doesn't care, and the other kids just watch him do whatever he wants to me. I'm going to get in so much trouble tomorrow in math! (Begins to cry.)

Dad: (Puts his hand gently on his son's shoulder and makes eye contact.) That's a lot to handle. I'm starting to understand why you are so upset. I'd like to know more details so that we can try to work things out. Can you start from the beginning and tell me how this started?

Ray: (Shrugs his shoulders. Looks defeated yet grateful for his father's quiet reassurance.)

Step 2: Use the Timeline to help a child put language to his emotions.

Dad: What happened in math today that made you think you're going to be in trouble?

Ray: Nothing happened in math. Math was fine. But it's going to be terrible tomorrow. I'm going to get in a ton of trouble, and it's all Nate's fault, but no one will believe me.

Dad: It's a terrible feeling to think that you won't be believed. I want to hear the truth about what happened. To start with, who is Nate?

Ray: He's a 10th grader, and he's such a jerk! He picks on me for no reason, and he always gets away with it. I hate him.

Dad: It sounds like this problem isn't about math as much as it is about Nate. What happened with Nate today?

Ray: It's not just today. It's every single day with that kid!

Dad: Having to deal with a difficult kid every single day can be so hard.

Ray: It is! It's so hard!

Dad: What has been going on with him?

Ray: He makes fun of me every day on the bus. He pushes me out of my seat. He takes my stuff. He calls me names. Yesterday, he stole my headphones and wouldn't give them back the whole ride. Today, he grabbed my math homework, ripped it up, and then threw it out the window. It took me the whole ride to get the homework done, and now it's completely gone. I'm going to get in so much trouble tomorrow.

Dad: Wow—that's a lot! Let me just make sure I have all of this straight. So, this 10th grader named Nate has been picking on you for a while now. He's been calling you names, pushing you, and taking your stuff. Today, he took your math homework and ripped it up. Then, he threw it out the window. You're worried that you're going to get in trouble tomorrow in math for not having your homework. I can definitely understand why you were feeling so upset when you got home!

Ray: I hate him so much. He never leaves me alone.

Dad: Dealing with an older kid who is pushing you around and messing with your things would be hard for anyone to handle. I'm really sorry this has been happening to you for so long. I'm also really glad that you are telling me about it because now that I know, I can help you figure out what to do about it. Is there anything else I need to know about your day or what's been going on with Nate?

Ray: That's pretty much it. Happens every day.

Step 3: Understand the problem—recognize the dynamics of displacement.

Dad: OK. So, let's think about what happened today. You're dealing with a really mean kid on the bus ride home every day. Today was an especially bad day because he destroyed the math homework that you worked hard on, and you won't have anything to turn in tomorrow in class. You are worried that you are going to get in trouble.

Ray: Yep.

Dad: So really, there are a few problems happening all at once. There's dealing with Nate, and there's dealing with your math teacher tomorrow.

Ray: Right—and it's not even my fault!

Dad: Things are feeling out of your control between this bigger kid that takes your stuff and your math teacher who might be angry that you don't have your homework.

Ray: Exactly! What am I supposed to do?

Dad: That's a good question. And I can help you figure out a good answer for what to do about Nate and how to talk to your math teacher about what's happened to your homework.

Ray: Thank you. Maybe you could talk to my bus driver and email my teacher?

Dad: I can definitely help you with both of those situations. But before we get to those things, there's one more problem from today that I think is important for us to work out. Do you know what it is?

Ray: (Looks confused.)

Dad: We need to talk about what happened between you and me—and the kitchen table. (Smiles.)

Ray: I was just so mad!

Dad: You swore at me and kicked the table.

Ray: I know. I'm sorry about that.

Dad: Thank you for apologizing. That shows a lot of maturity on your part. Now that you've told me about your day, understand that you weren't really angry at me. Your anger has to do with someone else.

Ray: Yeah—Nate!

Dad: Right. You were angry with Nate, and that is completely understandable. You felt like you couldn't do anything about your anger when you were on the bus, so instead, who got your anger?

Ray: You did. The kitchen table did.

Dad: That's right. Can you think of any other times when this kind of thing has happened? When you've been angry at one person and taken it out on someone else?

Ray: It happened two days ago after I got mad at Nate for making fun of me on the bus in the morning. When I got to school, I called my friend the same names that Nate called me. He got so mad that he told the teacher, and I lost recess.

Dad: Ray, listen closely. I understand why you have been feeling angry lately. What Nate has been doing to you is wrong, and you have every right to be upset about it. I will help you figure out what to do about Nate. But even before we do that, we need to do something about the fact that when you take your anger out on friends at school or family at home, you create a whole new set of problems.

Ray: I never thought about it like that.

Dad: And the worst part about it is that the people you are taking your anger out on are exactly the people you need to have on your side when you are dealing with people like Nate. Does that make sense?

Ray: Yeah. After I teased my friend in school, he hasn't talked to me since.

Dad: That's the problem with taking anger out on people who don't deserve it. We create new problems in addition to our old ones and push away the people who could help us.

Ray: (Nods in understanding, then responds defensively.) I hate Nate.

Step 4: Teach your child new skills for expressing his anger constructively.

Dad: So, what can you do to turn around this problem of taking your anger out on the wrong people?

Ray: Well, I could take it out on the right person instead! I could punch Nate next time he messes with me. Or steal his homework. Or take his whole backpack and throw it out the bus window.

Dad: I understand that that might feel good in the moment. But the problem is that getting revenge also causes new problems. If you punch Nate or throw his backpack out the window, you sink to his level and risk getting yourself in a lot of trouble. I promise that we're going to talk about Nate and about your math homework, but first, let's settle the issue of taking out your anger on the people who are actually on your side. What do you think you can do about this?

Ray: I have no idea.

Dad: Well, let me tell you what works for me. When I get really mad at someone, it helps me to get a cold drink of water to cool down my insides. Then, I usually need to just walk away from the situation for at least 10 minutes. I like to be by myself to just calm my brain—maybe listen to music or take a walk if it's nice outside. When I feel completely calm, it helps to try to talk to someone about the problem.

Ray: I do like to listen to music. And drawing really helps me calm down.

Dad: Those are both great ideas.

Ray: But I'm never going to be able to talk to Nate about how I feel. He'll just make fun of me more.

Dad: You're probably right. Telling Nate how you feel probably won't do a whole lot of good because he doesn't sound like a trustworthy person who would be willing to listen to you. Can you think of any people who are trustworthy who would listen and try to help you out?

Ray: You?

Dad: Absolutely. I'll listen to you and try to help you any day. Is there anyone at school you can talk to if Nate bothers you in the morning?

Ray: Mrs. McIntyre is pretty nice. She usually has time to talk.

Dad: That sounds like a good option. Would it be helpful if I called Mrs. McIntyre and told her a bit about what's been going on with Nate? Maybe together we can make a plan for how to deal with him.

Ray: You can call her, but I don't want Nate to know that I said anything. He'll call me a tattletale, and things will get even worse.

Dad: How about if you, me, and Mrs. McIntyre all sit down together to talk about what's been happening and come up with a plan to deal with Nate that doesn't end up making things worse for you?

Ray: That would be great! (Pauses.) What about my math homework?

Dad: What do you think we should do?

Ray: Maybe I can try to talk to my teacher before class and explain what happened. If he can give me another handout with the problems, I can get the assignment done.

Dad: I think that sounds like a solid plan. How are you feeling now?

Ray: Better. A little nervous about Nate still, but I feel better having a plan and having you on my side to help.

LSCI Skills in Practice

Ray's dad systematically guided his son through this SOS conversation and turned a problem situation into a skill-building opportunity. Notice that the father and son carried on a two-way dialog all the way through the process. At no time did Ray's father lecture, threaten, or dominate the conversation. The 4-step LSCI process works precisely because it is a back-and-forth process that allows a young person to feel heard, understood, and valued . What's more, because the young person is involved in understanding his problem and suggesting solutions, he gains invaluable problem-solving experience.

After using Drain-Off skills to reduce the intensity of Ray's anger, the father used Timeline skills to help his son tell his story and begin to make sense of the problem. Because of his careful building of a Timeline, Ray's father was able to realize that his son's anger at Nate had been displaced onto him. With this new knowledge, the father could then help his son understand what went wrong and how to more effectively manage anger in future situations so that potential helpers are not pushed away.

The displacement of anger is one of the most commonly identified self-defeating patterns of behavior in children. Chances are good that, as you have been reading this chapter, you have recalled a time or two in which your child displaced anger onto you (or perhaps a time that you displaced anger onto your child) and the conflict grew from there. When parents and caregivers understand the dynamic of displacement and are able to recognize it early on in a problem situation with their child, they can avoid becoming entangled in no-win power struggles that damage the parent–child relationship. The 4-step process guides adults and kids through conflict and toward more constructive ways to express anger.

> The 4-step LSCI process works precisely because it is a back-and-forth process that allows a young person to feel heard, understood, and valued.

You don't have to wait for an SOS crisis to occur in your family in order to make use of this new skill. Books, TV programs, and movies often portray incidents of displaced anger and can be a great source of nonthreatening discussion with kids about the impact of displacement on relationships. Non-conflict times provide ideal opportunities for parents and caregivers to teach kids skills for constructive anger expression. For example, you can:

- Encourage young children to draw pictures about ways to handle anger in healthy ways.

- Challenge upper elementary and middle school kids to cut pictures from magazines and create collages that have to do with handling anger.

- Engage teenagers in identifying common anger triggers and practicing skills for managing those situations when they inevitably arise.

- Introduce kids at any age to basic mindfulness practices that help regulate the brain. Movement and deep breathing are the go-to strategies for soothing an upset mind.

Preview of the Next Chapter

In the next chapter, we will explore stressful situations in which kids misperceive reality or have tunnel vision when it comes to their own point of view. You will learn skills for helping kids understand and accept alternate points of view during stressful situations.

CHAPTER 6

THE REALITY CHECK INTERVENTION
Clarifying Perceptions of Reality

Devon did not complete her weekly chores and therefore is not allowed to attend a sleepover at her friend's house on Friday night. Though she received daily reminders from her mother and is bright enough to understand that she did not meet her weekly responsibilities, she is furious with her mother for enforcing the no-sleepover consequence. Devon screams at her mother:

- "You never let me do anything."
- "You are so unfair! I hate you."
- "You just didn't want me to sleep over at Kelly's, and that's why you're making this whole thing up."

Devon's heartfelt belief is that her mother set her up for failure.

Devon's mother couldn't believe her ears. She didn't know if she should scream back at her daughter for lying, punish her for her disrespect, or take her to the doctor to have her head examined for the way she was perceiving the incident. *"How can she possibly twist this into being my fault?"* the mother wondered aloud.

There are times when the way our kids view a situation is just so different from how we view it that we wonder if we are even talking about the same thing. In these instances, it's tempting to conclude that they are just being difficult, or worse, is outright lying. Without a doubt, there are times when

> Stress, anxiety, anger, and fear of failure are just a few of the reasons why young people tend to get stuck—and stay stuck—in rigid patterns of perceiving the world.

people (of all ages) purposely bend the truth in order to avoid getting in trouble. However, it is also certain that *people perceive differently*. Stress, anxiety, anger, and fear of failure are just a few of the reasons why young people tend to get stuck—and stay stuck—in rigid patterns of perceiving the world.

The *Reality Check* intervention is designed to be used with young people who misperceive reality when their emotions unduly influence the way they interpret situations. This common self-defeating pattern of behavior is a major cause of conflict between adults and kids and can pose a significant challenge to healthy relationships. Parents and caregivers play a vital role in helping their kids consider new ways of thinking about problem situations and overcoming the tendency to let emotion color their reality.

What Do You See?

One of the very best ways to help young people understand that *people perceive differently* and come to realize that there is more than one way to view a situation is to use concrete images, such as the one featured in Chapter 1 or the one below.

If you take the perspective of the man on the left, you likely see the number 6. If you are looking from the point of view of the man on the right, you probably see the number 9 (or a lowercase letter g). The men appear to be irritated with one another and seem to be insisting that their perception is the right perception. In fact, they are both correct.

How can it be that two people can look at the same thing, perceive it differently, and yet both still be 100 percent correct? The Reality Check intervention is designed to shed light on this question.

Returning briefly to the information from Chapter 1, we know that when the amygdala is activated, it takes over a young person's ability to fully access her neocortex. In other words, during stressful situations, kids are driven by emotions rather than logic and language. When Devon realizes she has lost her privilege to have a sleepover at her friend's house, her overwhelming disappointment and frustration activate her amygdala and impair her ability to logically connect her actions (failure to complete her chores) with their consequences (not having a sleepover.) In the heat of the moment, the only conclusion Devon is able to make is that her mother must be cruel and unjust. No matter how farfetched Devon's version of reality seems to her mother, keep in mind that for Devon—stuck in the stress of the situation—her way of perceiving the situation is as certain as your perception of the number 9 (or the letter g) in the image above.

Misperceiving Events in a Reality Check Situation

The Reality Check intervention is used by parents and caregivers to help young people clarify reality and identify new ways of perceiving their world. It is based on the understanding that, during stressful situations, young people hear things, see things, and interpret things not necessarily as they are but as they believe them to be (Long, Wood, & Fecser, 2001). The Reality Check approach to parent–child conflict acknowledges that even when caregivers and kids perceive a situation differently, it doesn't mean that either person is wrong. Rather, because *people perceive differently*, both viewpoints may have some degree of validity. The Timeline skills used in LSCI's 4-step process are the perfect tool to help adults and kids learn about each other's point of view.

The 4-Step Process at Work in a Reality Check Situation

The ultimate goal of the Reality Check is to improve the parent–child relationship by providing a framework for talking through opposing perceptions of a conflict situation. Read on to learn how LSCI's 4-steps can guide you to clarifying differing perceptions of reality for you and your child.

> Note that the steps below follow the same framework as the ones used to address the dynamic of displacement in the SOS intervention (Chapter 5). Throughout this book, we use a consistent 4-step process to help you work through parent–child conflict and help kids overcome self-defeating patterns of behavior. Having a framework to follow is helpful because:

- Parents and caregivers can rely on a familiar process, rather than freezing up and not knowing how to respond, when their children present a new, troubling behavior.

- Kids benefit from having a consistent and structured pattern of responses from their parents. This steadiness and predictability gives young people a sense of safety and helps build trust with caregivers. Safety and trust are both prerequisites for healthy bonds between adults and children.

Step 1: Use the process of Drain Off to help the young person reduce the intensity of her emotions.

- Your first priority is to drain off the intensity of your child's feelings. Be sure to maintain your own calm and composure, as the steadiness of your demeanor can have a soothing effect on your child's emotional state.

- Use the five core listening skills described in Chapter 2 to help your child feel heard, understood, and valued.

- Recognize that people perceive differently. If your child's version of reality is very different from yours, refrain from jumping to the conclusion that she is lying or being difficult. Instead, consider the very real possibility that the stress of the moment has colored her thinking and that, in the moment, her perception is her reality. Your ultimate task is to clarify her perception of reality and help her consider that alternate perceptions can coexist.

> Your ultimate task is to clarify her perception of reality and help her consider that alternate perceptions can coexist.

Step 2: Use the Timeline to help the child put language to her emotions.

- Once the young person's intense emotions are thoroughly drained off, use the Timeline skills (see Chapter 3) to help her put words to her feelings and begin to engage the problem-solving part of her brain.

- In order to find out if a isperception of reality is the cause of the problem, it is helpful to ask questions that help a child clarify the events leading up to the problem situation. Through your questions, help the young person connect causes with effects and personal actions with resulting consequences.

> Through your questions, help the young person connect causes with effects and personal actions with resulting consequences.

- The Conflict Cycle (see Chapter 1) is an especially helpful tool in the Reality Check intervention. Use a visual of the Conflict Cycle—or sketch one out on paper—to show a child, step-by-step, how stress influences perceptions, which influence thoughts, feelings, behaviors, and others' reactions. With the Conflict Cycle as your guide, use Timeline questions to reconstruct the events leading up to the incident to help your child bring logical order to her emotional memory of the incident. As such, she has the opportunity to understand how her behavior played a role in the problem and how to avoid making the same mistake again in the future.

- To be effective, the Timeline step must be carried out in a nonjudgmental way. The Timeline is not about proving that your perception is right and the child's way of perceiving is wrong. Rather, it is about helping the child clarify her perceptions of what happened and consider alternate conclusions.

- You will know you are ready to move on to Step 3 of the process when the child's emotional state remains calm; she has been able to use words to describe her perceptions, thoughts, and feelings about what happened; and you both have a clearer understanding of the events that have taken place.

    o If you do not feel completely clear on the Timeline of events or if your child still seems to be struggling to make sense out of the situation, continue to ask Timeline questions to gain clarity. Do not be discouraged if it takes awhile to get all of the details or to understand your child's point of view. You are not doing anything wrong! The more intense the emotion of the situation, the longer it often takes to make good sense of it.

    o A helpful way to transition from Step 2 to Step 3 is to summarize the young person's story from beginning to end. In doing so, you show the child that you have truly listened and paid attention to her point of view. What's more, hearing about the problem situation in someone else's words assists the child in gaining needed clarity about the events.

Step 3: Understand the problem—recognize the misperception of reality.

- Once the young person's perception of the situation has been clarified using Step 2, it is time to shift your focus from information gathering to understanding the problem.

- Begin Step 3 by asking the young person questions to help her consider new or different ways of thinking about the events leading up to the problem situation. Again, this is not a "Your way is wrong, my way is right" conversation but rather an "Is it possible that there is another way of looking at this?" discussion.

- In Step 3, the adult's goal is to clarify the child's perception of reality, while at the same time helping her consider that alternate perceptions also exist. In shedding light on multiple points of view, you help your child understand that people perceive differently and that being willing to consider someone else's point of view is a critical part of resolving conflict.

- In any situation where an adult's and a child's perceptions differ, it is common for adults to take on an authoritarian role, where they insist that their way of perceiving is the only right way of perceiving. The problem, of course, is that the child has the exact same belief—that her perception is the only right perception! To genuinely help children, parents and caregivers must:

    1. Acknowledge that people perceive differently.

    2. Shed light on multiple points of view instead of insisting on just one version of reality.

Step 4: Teach your child new skills for considering alternate points of view.

- Step 4 is a skill-building stage. Here, rather than punishing a child for her way of perceiving reality, you have the opportunity to teach her the skills she needs to consider alternate points of view in future conflict situations. In a Reality Check situation, teaching kids skills to consider alternate ways of perceiving reality is essential.

- Step 4 is completed when both you and your child feel satisfied that the problem situation has been discussed, a new possible

> In a Reality Check situation, teaching kids skills to consider alternate ways of perceiving reality is essential.

understanding of reality has emerged, and the young person feels better equipped with strategies to manage differing perceptions of the same reality the next time a similar situation occurs.

What If My Child's Perception Is Wrong?

The Reality Check intervention is the perfect approach for helping young people whose emotions have colored their perception of an event because it acknowledges that "to the corkscrew, the knife looks crooked." In other words, the Reality Check works because it accepts the fact that people perceive differently and that *each person's perception is their reality during the heat of the moment.*

Each person's perception is their reality during the heat of the moment.

It is important to note that accepting differences in perception is not the same thing as taking each person's statement as absolute truth. Because we know that, during stressful situations, kids are dominated by their emotional brain, we understand that their perceptions are not always grounded in logic and reason. That's a scientific way of explaining that sometimes a child's perception of an event is wrong. The Reality Check approach works not because it zeroes in on a single correct interpretation of events but rather because:

1. It allows the young person's version of events to be put into words and acknowledged by a caring adult.

2. The very act of talking about the event helps kids gain clarity on things like cause and effect, actions, and consequences.

3. Timeline questions open up new possibilities for interpreting situations, and kids begin to understand that there may be *more than one way* to perceive an event.

4. When an adult acknowledges the young person's way of perceiving, she becomes more willing to acknowledge that the adult has a valid way of perceiving the event as well.

5. The experience of realizing that people perceive differently opens kids up to considering alternate perspectives in future situations.

Bottom line: Even though a young person's perception of an event may be wrong, it will do you no good to tell her this in the heat of the moment or to refuse to even listen to her version of reality. At best, shutting down conversation misses the opportunity to help a young person develop skills to consider new ways of perceiving. At worst, refusing to listen to your child's point of view makes her feel worthless and causes damage to the parent–child relationship in the long term.

> **When an adult acknowledges the young person's way of perceiving, she becomes more willing to acknowledge that the adult has a valid way of perceiving the event as well.**

The 4-Step Process With Devon and Her Mother

In the pages that follow, we offer you an example of what an LSCI Reality Check intervention between Devon and her mother could sound like using the 4-step process. Remember that there is no "script" to an LSCI intervention. Your conversation with your child does not have to sound precisely like our example. We encourage you to learn from the structure and the key phrases we use but to always maintain your own authenticity in your interactions with a young person.

Use the example below as a general guide that provides:

Step 1: Useful phrases for Drain Off
Step 2: Effective Timeline questions using the Conflict Cycle as a visual guide
Step 3: Helpful ways to gain a new understanding of the problem
Step 4: Practical skills for managing different perceptions in conflict-free ways

Step 1: Use the process of Drain Off to help a child reduce the intensity of her emotions.

Devon: (Yelling) You just don't want me to sleep over at Kelly's. That's what this is about.

Mom: (Sits down in a chair to try to bring down the level of tension in the room. Uses a steady voice and makes direct but gentle eye contact.) You think I want to ruin your fun.

Devon: (Still pacing) Yeah, this is so completely unfair!

Mom: You are angry because you feel like you aren't being treated fairly.

Devon: I'm not! You never let me do anything.

Mom: I can see that you are really disappointed right now and really upset with me. Having to cancel plans with friends never feels good.

Devon: Well, we don't have to cancel the plans then! You can just let me go like you said I could on Monday!

Mom: You are right that we did talk on Monday about you sleeping over at Kelly's.

Devon: Yeah, and you said I could do it, and now you're taking it back. You're such a liar!

Mom: (Feels her face get red and hot. Feels angry at being called a liar by her daughter. Takes a slow, deep breath to keep herself from reacting angrily.) Calling me a liar is not going to help us figure this out. Let's see if we can sit here together and try to talk about the sleepover in a respectful way. Are you willing to do that?

Devon: (Stops pacing. Throws herself into the sofa with her back turned to her mother.) Fine.

Mom: Thank you.

Step 2: Use the Timeline to help Devon put language to her emotions.

Mom: You are absolutely right that on Monday when you asked me if you could sleep over at Kelly's house this weekend that I said that you could go.

Devon: See! You admit it. You said I could, and now you won't let me. You're being unfair!

Mom: I did say that you could. You're correct. (Pauses briefly.) Do you remember what else I said when you asked me about the sleepover?

Devon: Yeah. You said that I had to be home in time to get ready for my soccer game on Saturday.

Mom:	Right. We talked about you needing to get home, eat lunch, and change before your soccer game. I'm glad you remembered that detail. Do you remember what else we talked about?
Devon:	I don't know.
Mom:	Before we talked about soccer, I told you that the clothes on your floor would have to be picked up and that you needed to vacuum your room. Does that sound familiar?
Devon:	(Insistent) Well, yeah, but I didn't know I had to do those things before I slept over. Why can't I just do it when I get home from Kelly's? It's my room!
Mom:	It is your room—I won't argue with you about that. And most of the time, I let you keep it the way you want. But our family rule has always been that once a week, you and your brother have to pick up all of the stuff you leave on the floor and make sure your room is vacuumed. This is not a new rule.
Devon:	(Sensing a loophole in the family rule) But why do I have to do it before I go to Kelly's? You're just trying to make it so that I can't sleep over at her house! We already figured out plans for what we're going to do tonight, and Kelly is going to be so mad. You are ruining her night too!
Mom:	In your mind, I am the cause of the problem you are having. I have a—
Devon:	(Interrupts.) You are the cause of my problem! You are the cause of Kelly's problem too!
Mom:	I have a different way of thinking about this situation. Can we look at something together for a minute? I need you to help me

	make sure that I am remembering this week accurately. Sometimes I get busy and forget things, so I want to make sure that didn't happen.
Devon:	Sure. I think you probably are forgetting something! Like, that you said I could sleep over.
Mom:	It's possible that I did forget something. Let's see if we can figure this out together. (Draws a quick diagram of the Conflict Cycle on a piece of paper, starting with the circle at the top, which represents the stressful event.) OK. So, can we agree that on Monday, you asked me if you could sleep over at Kelly's house this Friday night?
Devon:	Yes. And you said that I could.
Mom:	Right. What else did I say? (Fills in the Conflict Cycle as details are discussed.)
Devon:	You said my chores had to be done.
Mom:	Right. And what did you say?
Devon:	I said "OK. Great!" And I was super excited, so I texted Kelly to tell her that I could sleep over.
Mom:	I'm glad we are in agreement so far. This is helpful to me. So, did you clean your room right away?
Devon:	No. I never clean it on Mondays!
Mom:	Ahh. OK. Maybe you were thinking you still had plenty of time to get it done before the sleepover?

Devon:	I wasn't actually thinking about it at all. I was just excited about the sleepover.
Mom:	I can understand that. I used to love sleepovers too and remember looking forward to them all week.
Devon:	It's all we talked about at school all week long.
Mom:	So, the sleepover was on your mind all week. I did notice you were in a really good mood every day after school, which I love seeing. On Wednesday night, I reminded you that your room needed to be picked up and vacuumed before the sleepover. Do you remember me telling you that?
Devon:	Yeah—you almost came into my room when I was getting dressed for soccer.
Mom:	That's right. I was about to walk in, but you told me to stop. I just reminded you from the doorway. Do you remember what you said?
Devon:	I think I just said, "I will!"
Mom:	That's what I remember too. Did you clean your room that night?
Devon:	No. I was busy with soccer practice.
Mom:	OK. Do you remember thinking about when you would have time to do your chores?
Devon:	Not really. I wasn't thinking about it. I was thinking about soccer and school stuff.

Mom: OK. I see. You were thinking about the things you had going on that night and weren't paying as much attention to things that would need to be done later in the week.

Devon: I guess.

Mom: Do you remember what you were thinking last night when I reminded you again?

Devon: I was in the middle of packing for Kelly's. I think I thought I'd just put everything from my floor into my overnight bag and then wouldn't have to worry about cleaning the floor.

Mom: (Laughs.) That's definitely one way to get clothing off of your floor. I might have done the same thing a time or two when I was your age.

Devon: (Smiles at her mother.)

Mom: So, you did have a strategy for getting that part of your chore done. Did you have a strategy for vacuuming?

Devon: Not really. I wasn't thinking about that part.

Mom: That part of the chore slipped your mind.

Devon: I guess. I mean, I do it every week, so I sort of think about it by habit, but I don't know—I think the time just sort of flew by this week, and I forgot.

Mom: The time flew by this week for me too. I can understand forgetting. (Looks back at the paper with the notes she has written from the Conflict Cycle. Points at each item to summarize

	what they have discussed so far.) So, let me just make sure I'm not forgetting anything here. We agree that on Monday you asked me if you could have a sleepover at Kelly's. I said you could as long as your chores were done. You said OK to this and were feeling really excited. You had a busy week and were focused on things like the sleepover, soccer, and schoolwork. You said you weren't thinking about your household chores. I realized this was probably the case, so I gave you a few reminders about getting your chores done before the sleepover. You remember me doing this but also remember being busy at the time. Is that all correct so far?
Devon:	Yeah.
Mom:	Am I forgetting anything up to this point?
Devon:	I don't think so.
Mom:	Good. OK. So now it's Friday, and you are wanting me to drive you to Kelly's. I told you that since your chore never got finished, the sleepover could not happen. Now, you are feeling really angry at me about this and have been telling me that I am the cause of your problem. You said that you think I just don't want you to sleep over at Kelly's.
Devon:	Exactly. You don't! You're just trying to make it so that I can't sleep over at her house!
Mom:	In your mind, this is my fault.
Devon:	It is. You are ruining my night and Kelly's night too!
Mom:	Devon, I understand that you were really counting on the sleepover. I feel badly that Kelly's night is going to be affected by this, and I feel badly for you too because I know how much you

	want to go. Nevertheless, the rule I gave you was that your room had to be clean before the sleepover.
Devon:	If you really felt bad, you'd change the rule and let me go!

Step 3: Understand the problem—recognize the misperception of reality.

Mom:	To be honest with you, Devon, it would be easy for me to change the rule. You would get to have your sleepover, and I wouldn't have my daughter being so angry. We might both even feel better in a way.
Devon:	Exactly. So, change the rule!
Mom:	The thing is, you are focusing only on the privilege you want to have and disregarding the responsibility you need to carry out in order to earn the privilege.
Devon:	(Pauses.) So?
Mom:	So, I can totally understand where you are coming from that you want me to change the rule in order for you to have your privilege.
Devon:	Awesome! So, I can go?
Mom:	I'm wondering if there is a part of you that can understand where I am coming from when I remind you that you earn privileges, such as sleeping over at Kelly's, by carrying out responsibilities.
Devon:	I do understand that, but I just don't understand why you can't make an exception to the rule this one time.

Mom: (Feels her anger rising once again as her daughter persists and persists. Takes another deep breath and exhales slowly.) Devon, I admire your persistence. It will suit you well someday if you want to be a lawyer. In this case, though, you are not arguing for justice. You are arguing to get your way in a situation even when you know you have not held up your responsibility. I'm not asking you to be happy about my decision, but I am asking you to consider that your actions played a role in my decision, and I am not just canceling the sleepover to be mean or because I'm out to get you. Does that make sense?

Devon: Fine. I get it. I didn't finish cleaning my room when I was supposed to. I'm sorry!

Mom: Thank you for the apology. I am glad we could talk about this together without fighting. I appreciate your willingness to try to understand where I'm coming from.

Step 4: Teach your child new skills for perceiving situations from multiple perspectives.

Devon: If I finish cleaning it now, can I still go?

Mom: The sleepover is canceled for tonight. If you are invited again and you have your chores done in time, you can go then.

Devon: Fine. (Gets up to leave the room.)

Mom: Devon, on Monday when you asked me about the sleepover, I told you the rules. Then, I reminded you two other times this week.

Devon: I know! Don't rub it in.

Mom:	I'm sorry for the way that sounded. I'm not trying to rub anything in. What I want to know is, how can I help you stay organized with things like chores, homework, and other responsibilities, even when you are busy with school and soccer? Would it help for me to put deadlines on the calendar in the kitchen?
Devon:	I don't think so. I never really look at that calendar. (Pauses). Maybe I could set reminders on my phone.
Mom:	That's a great idea. You always have your phone with you, so that sounds like a really good way to remind yourself of what needs to be done. Can I help in any other way?
Devon:	Maybe you could write down any of the chores I have to do and give me the list at the beginning of the week. Then, I can put them on my phone.
Mom:	That sounds like a really solid plan. I'm willing to help you stay organized and keep up with your responsibilities. I'm on your side and want you to be able to enjoy privileges like sleepovers. I also need you to know that it's up to you to complete the responsibilities and live with the consequences of not completing them.
Devon:	Well, I'm definitely learning that right now. I have to go text Kelly.
Mom:	OK. Thank you again for talking this through with me.
Devon:	You're welcome.

LSCI Skills in Practice

Devon's mother skillfully navigated the waters of this potentially explosive conflict with her daughter using the Reality Check intervention to turn Devon's one-sided perception of events into a skill-building opportunity. The mother was particularly effective in maintaining her composure throughout the conversation, using self-calming skills whenever she began to feel herself reacting emotionally to Devon's name-calling, accusations, and insistence on her own version of the truth. Let's imagine how the conversation might have played out if the mother had allowed herself to take her daughter's emotional bait and become carried away by anger:

Devon: *(Yelling) You just don't want me to sleep over at Kelly's. That's what this is about.*

Mom: *(Walks closer to Devon. Raises her voice to the level of Devon's and glares at her daughter.) Oh, so now you're blaming me!*

Devon: *Yeah! This is so completely unfair!*

Mom: *You didn't finish cleaning your room, and you're telling me that I'm unfair? You better think again!*

Devon: *You never let me do anything.*

Mom: *I let you do everything you want! Maybe that's the problem—maybe you're too used to getting to do everything you want without having to work for it. How about if we cancel all sleepovers for the next month? How about if I add in new chores every week so that you can take some real responsibility around here!*

Devon: *Fine! I don't care if I never have a sleepover again. I hate you!*

Or, consider how Devon's mother could have escalated the conflict and derailed the learning opportunity if she had taken her daughter's name-calling bait:

Mom: *You are right that we did talk on Monday about you sleeping over at Kelly's.*

Devon: *Yeah, and you said I could do it, and now you're taking it back. You're such a liar!*

Mom: *(Feels her face get red and hot. Feels angry at being called a liar by her daughter. Stands up from her chair and stands two inches from her daughter.) Are you calling me the liar in this situation?*

Devon: *(Feels cornered.) Yes.*

Mom: *You're the liar! You lied when you said you'd clean your room, and you're lying again now to try to get what you want. You're sneaky, but you're not going to get away with it. You are grounded all weekend. No phone either! Go up to your room.*

In both of the conversations above, Devon's mother allows her emotional brain to dictate her reactions to her daughter. In neither example did the mother and daughter reach a higher level of mutual understanding or strengthen their relationship in any way. Rather, in accepting her daughter's invitation to argue, the mom missed the opportunity to role-model calming skills and respectful communication—not to mention giving Devon the chance to understand the problem from a new perspective.

Returning to a review of the conversation as it originally played out, after effectively using Drain-Off skills during Step 1 to reduce the intensity of Devon's feelings, the mother initiated Timeline skills. In this step, the mother helped her daughter expand her perspective from a one-sided focus on the loss of her privilege to a broader acknowledgment of her household responsibilities. Note some of the language the mother used to make Devon feel heard and to acknowledge the validity of Devon's perception of events:

- You are absolutely right that...
- I did say that you could. You're correct...

- It is your room—I won't argue with you about that…
- I understand that you were really counting on the sleepover…

While consistently acknowledging Devon's perception, the mother skillfully asserted her point of view as well, showing her daughter that two different perceptions can coexist:

- Before we talked about soccer, I told you that the clothes on your floor would have to be picked up and that you needed to vacuum your room. Does that sound familiar?

- Nevertheless, the rule I gave you was that your room had to be clean before the sleepover.

Devon's mother made use of the Conflict Cycle as a guide to help her daughter think through the events of the week and make the connection between her failure to finish cleaning her room and her loss of the sleepover. Through this visual guide, Devon was prepared for the new understanding developed in Step 3 that her own behavior—not her mother's—led to the cancelation of her privilege.

Devon's mother used Step 3 to highlight both her perspective and Devon's perspective, without calling either one "right" or "wrong." Key phrases such as "I'm wondering if there is a part of you that…" are especially helpful in the Reality Check.

Also in Step 3, note how Devon's mother sidesteps her daughter's insistence on getting her way by affirming her persistence as a skill ("Devon, I admire your persistence") while still remaining steadfast. This affirmation brings down the level of conflict and paves the path for further conversation.

Sometimes, after using an intervention like the Reality Check and helping kids gain new insights, parents may want to reward their children for taking part in the feel-good conversation. Although we would never argue against the feeling of goodwill with your child, we applaud the way Devon's mother held fast to the consequence of losing the sleepover while still teaching her how to avoid the loss of privilege in the future.

You don't have to wait for a Reality Check crisis to occur in your family in order to make use of this new skill. Consider these ideas for helping your young person clarify perspectives and accept multiple ways of perceiving the world.

- Engage kids in conversation about times when they had a different opinion or point of view than a friend or relative. You may want to share times when your perception of reality differed from someone else's and how you went about finding common ground—or just agreeing to disagree. The more realistic and relatable your example, the better.

- The Internet is a great place to find optical illusions and images that can be perceived differently, such as the duck/rabbit image in Chapter 1 or the numbers cartoon in this chapter. Use a search engine and key phrases such as "horse frog illusion" or "perspective pictures old lady" to get started in finding examples. Use these images with kids as a fun way of practicing the skill of looking for alternate ways of perceiving.

- Make it a habit when talking about friendship issues to challenge your child to consider what each person might be thinking or how they might perceive an event. This is a great way to get kids accustomed to the idea that people perceive differently and that different perspectives can be equally correct.

Preview of the Next Chapter

In the next chapter, we will examine stressful situations in which kids want to do the right thing behaviorally, socially, or academically but lack the social skills to know how to do so. Parents and caregivers will learn skills for helping kids understand social cues and respond in prosocial ways.

CHAPTER 7

THE NEW TOOLS INTERVENTION
Teaching New Social Skills

Chris wants to play with his brothers Eddie and Mike. While Eddie and Mike are playing a video game, Chris reaches over, grabs Mike's game controller, and starts to control his character. In Chris's mind, he is trying to help Mike get to the next level. In Mike's mind, Chris just stole his game controller and ruined his game. Mike punches Chris in the arm—hard!

Chris becomes upset. He tries to punch Mike back, but Eddie stops him. Both Eddie and Mike yell at Chris to leave their room. Chris is distraught. His arm hurts, and he feels confused, saddened, and rejected by his brothers. He approaches his mother for help with the situation.

Do you frequently find your child becoming frustrated and confused in social situations? Does he go into a situation with good intentions but come out of it with the wrong results? Are peer interactions a constant struggle and making friends a mystery?

For kids who frequently misunderstand interpersonal cues and lack appropriate social behaviors, daily life can feel like an endless series of frustrations, missteps, humiliations, and indignities. *The New Tools* intervention is designed to meet the needs of young people who want to do the right thing but find that things keep coming out wrong.

Right Idea Gone Wrong

As a parent or caregiver, can you relate to Chris's situation above or to any of the other New Tools incidents described below?

Scenario 1

Russell wants to be friends with the other kids in his neighborhood, but he always feels like he doesn't quite fit in. One afternoon, he steals money from his father's wallet and gives it to Jack, one of the most popular kids on the block, to try to seem "cool." When the other kids laugh at him for letting Jack take his money, Russell feels embarrassed and confused. When he gets in trouble with his father, he tearfully explains, "I was just trying to make a friend."

Scenario 2

Freddy often struggles in math, but he has been working extra hard and dedicating a lot of time to doing better in this class. When his mother looks through his school notebook and sees that he got a 100 percent on his recent math test, he jumps up on the kitchen table, starts dancing, and shouts, "I'm the smartest kid in the whole family!"

Scenario 3

Ten-year-old Ella admires her older brother, Jordan, and is always trying to figure out how to get him to pay attention to her. Thirteen-year-old Jordan prefers to be left alone. His bedroom is filled with models he has built by hand, and he always keeps his bedroom door closed so that no one messes with his creations. One day, Ella sneaks into Jordan's room and starts to rearrange small pieces in each model. She thinks this is a good way to make her brother laugh and can't wait until he gets home to see her prank. When Jordan gets home, he notices the changes to his models right away. However, instead of perceiving them as a funny joke, Jordan is furious. He runs to Ella's room where she is eagerly awaiting him. Instead of laughing, Jordan screams at Ella and threatens to break everything in her room if she ever touches his models again. Jordan slams her door and leaves his sister in tears and genuinely bewildered as to why her big brother didn't find her joke funny.

When young people have good intentions—trying to make a friend, succeeding academically, amusing a sibling—this is a wonderful thing. Most parents are thrilled when their kids want to do well. Learning socially appropriate ways to accomplish their worthy goals can be tricky for some young people, however. The New Tools intervention offers adults a framework for helping kids "do the right thing" in the "right" way.

It's important to note that misunderstanding interpersonal cues and societal rules is a common challenge for many children. Developmentally speaking, it is not at all uncommon for younger kids who interact with older peers to fall short when it comes to understanding acceptable social behaviors. Diagnostically, some children may be especially prone to social skill deficits, especially those who are on the autism spectrum. In either case, the good news is this: Behavior tends to be much easier to change than attitudes. If you have a child who genuinely wants to do the right thing, you are already ahead of the game!

The 4-Step Process at Work in a New Tools Situation

The ultimate goal of the New Tools approach is to help your child adopt more effective social behaviors. Read on to learn how LSCI's 4-step process can guide you to support your child's good intentions while teaching new social skills.

Step 1: Use the process of Drain Off to help Chris reduce the intensity of his emotion.

- As always, your priority is to drain off the intensity of your child's feelings. In addition to using the five core listening skills described in Chapter 2, parents can use calming behaviors, such as taking deep breaths or getting a cold drink of water, to role-model for kids how to soothe and regulate their emotional state.

- In a New Tools situation, a young person's anger or indignation may seem extreme at first. If the child's feelings are acknowledged and affirmed, however, usually they transform quickly into raw emotions of confusion or embarrassment.

- It is in seeing this emotional shift that you may first come to recognize that your child was motivated by positive intentions and is feeling upset that things didn't turn out as expected. Your ultimate task in a New Tools situation is to affirm his good ideas and teach him the new social skills he needs to achieve his worthy goals.

- In some ways, Drain Off in a New Tools situation may seem easier than in the other interventions we have reviewed so far. This is because the young person is "beyond active resistance" (Long, Wood, & Fecser, 2001). In other words, the child in this situation usually wants adult help to understand what went wrong.

- On the other hand, Step 1 can pose a real challenge for adults who become frustrated by a child's socially inappropriate behavior. A parent or caregiver might mistakenly believe their child is misbehaving on purpose. They may think the poor social behavior must be met with immediate punishment. The problem with this approach is that, although the young person might learn what behavior his parent doesn't like, he misses out on the opportunity to learn how to behave better in future situations. The advantage of the New Tools intervention—and other LSCI approaches—is that it replaces short-lived fixes such as punishment with long-lasting, positive behavioral changes through the teaching of new skills that can be relied upon over and over again by kids.

> The advantage of the New Tools intervention is that it replaces short-lived fixes such as punishment with long-lasting, positive behavioral changes by teaching new social skills.

Step 2: Use the Timeline to help Chris put language to emotions.

- Once Chris's anger at his brothers seems to be thoroughly drained off, it's a good indication that he is ready to begin engaging the problem-solving part of his brain.

- In order to find out if a misunderstanding of social behaviors—including video game etiquette—is the root issue, it is beneficial to ask questions that help Chris clarify the events leading up to the problem situation.

Using the Conflict Cycle as your guide, ask Chris questions to shed light on:

The LSCI Conflict Cycle

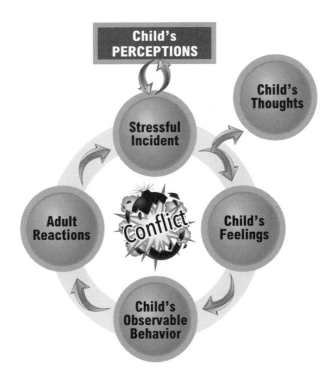

- What was happening? (e.g., the *stressful* event)
- What was he was *thinking* as he watched his brothers playing the game?
- What was he was feeling as he sat watching the game?
- What did he hope would happen when he grabbed the controller? (behavior)
- How did Mike and Eddie actually respond when he grabbed the controller? (This sibling reaction then became the next stressful event.)
- What was he thinking and feeling after Mike punched him?
- And so on ...

- The Conflict Cycle can be an extremely useful tool to help kids like Chris bring logical order to their emotional memory of an incident. In doing so, the child has the opportunity to learn how his good intentions were perceived negatively by others and created a problem he did not anticipate.

- The Conflict Cycle is equally useful to adults as they determine the core issue of a problem situation. As you will note below, it's not always easy to determine the real problem.

    o   Might this be an SOS situation in which Chris is bringing anger home from a school situation and taking it out on his brothers?
    o   Is there a Reality Check dynamic in which Chris misinterprets the reason Mike punched him?
    o   Is Chris's misunderstanding of taking turns and video game etiquette the essence of the problem?

Perhaps all three issues are at play; however, teaching kids three new ways to understand a problem all at once is never advised! The benefit of using the Conflict Cycle to guide your questions in Step 2 is that it can shed light on Chris's positive thoughts and intentions, which in turn can guide you to focus in on his misunderstanding of social situations as the core problem to solve.

Kids Will Be Kids?

In situations involving sibling conflict, it is important for parents and caregivers to avoid the urge to rush in and solve the problem right away. *Not doing something* may seem counterintuitive. True, it would be quick and easy for Chris's mom to jump into the situation, turn off the video game, punish Mike for punching Chris, and send the boys to separate spaces. Likewise, the incident could be resolved in a snap if the mother just told Chris that "boys will be boys" and dismissed his pleas for help. Either of these short-term solutions, however, would deprive Chris of the opportunity to understand where he went wrong with his brothers and how he could more effectively join in their play in the future. (And Mike would miss out on learning less aggressive ways of interacting.)

- You will know you are ready to move on to Step 3 of the process when Chris's emotional state remains calm, he has been able to talk about the events of the Conflict Cycle, and you both have a better understanding of how a right idea ended up going all wrong.

    o If you do not feel completely clear on the Timeline of events or if your child still seems to be struggling to make sense out of the situation, continue to ask Timeline questions to gain clarity. Do not be discouraged if it takes awhile to get all of the details or to understand your child's point of view—you are not doing anything wrong! The more intense the emotion of the situation, the longer it often takes to make good sense of it.

    o A helpful way to transition from Step 2 to Step 3 is to summarize the young person's story from beginning to end. In doing so, you show the child that you have truly listened and paid attention to his point of view. What's more, hearing about the problem situation in someone else's words assists the child in gaining needed clarity about the events.

Step 3: Understand the problem—recognize that Chris's intentions (to play with his brothers) were good, but the way he went about approaching them (stealing Mike's game controller) was unwise.

- Once Chris has had the opportunity to put his story into words using Step 2, it is time to shift your focus from information gathering to understanding the problem.

- Begin Step 3 by asking Chris questions that highlight his good intentions. The importance of this action cannot be overstated. The New Tools intervention will only be effective if parents and caregivers spend time affirming that the young

> The New Tools intervention will only be effective if parents and caregivers spend time affirming that the young person was trying to do the right thing.

person was trying to do the right thing. This fact is truly a big deal, and it is the foundation on which the rest of the intervention depends.

- Once the child's good intention (helping Mike get to the next level in his video game) has been established, the next step is to ask questions that help Chris understand which of his behaviors interfered with his positive goal. In gaining insight as to where he went wrong, Chris becomes open to learning about how he can behave differently in future situations.

Step 4: Teach your child new skills for considering alternate points of view.

- Step 4 is a skill-building stage. This step is important in all of the LSCI interventions, but it is emphasized in the New Tools approach

> In a New Tools situation, spending time teaching and practicing new social skills is essential.

because kids like Chris lack the appropriate social behaviors to accomplish their goals. In a New Tools situation, spending time teaching and practicing new social skills is essential.

- What is the most important social skill Chris needs to learn to be successful in this situation? There are probably a few that we could identify, but it's most helpful to pick just one or two behaviors that Chris can change. Focusing on too many new skills at once would be overwhelming and would likely decrease the effectiveness of the intervention. In the example below, we will focus on teaching Chris how to more effectively join his brothers at play.

- Step 4 is completed when you and Chris both feel satisfied that the problem situation has been discussed, a clear understanding of the events leading up to the problem has emerged, and Chris feels better equipped with strategies to manage similar social situations in the future.

The 4-Step Process With Chris and His Mother

In the pages that follow, we offer you an example of what an LSCI New Tools intervention between Chris and his mother might sound like using the 4-step process. Remember that there is no "script" to an LSCI intervention. Your conversation with your child does not have to sound precisely like our example. We encourage you to learn from the structure and the key phrases we use but to always maintain your own authenticity in your interactions with a young person.

Step 1: Use the process of Drain Off to help Chris reduce the intensity of his emotions.

Chris: (Walking into his mother's room) They are always ganging up on me!

I hate them both!

Mom: (Stands up to give Chris a hug.)

Chris: (Gives his mom a hug, then returns to being upset.) Can you please do something about Mike and Eddie? They are not letting me play! And Mike punched me really hard! (Rubs his arm where he was punched.)

Mom: Are you OK?

Chris: I'm fine. He can't hurt me. He's just mad because I'm better than him at his own game.

Mom: It looks like you're pretty mad right now too. Sounds like there's a lot going on with you and your brothers.

Chris: (Starts to cry.) I just don't know why they are always so mean to me. Why won't they let me play?

Mom: It's so hard to feel left out. I'm sorry you are hurting right now. Would you like some help trying to sort it all through?

Chris: I need you to make them let me play.

Mom: Let's see what we can do to make things better. Why don't you start by telling me what happened.

Step 2: Use the Timeline to help Chris bring language to emotions and talk about his intentions in taking the game controller.

Chris: Mike punched me in the arm because he's so jealous that I'm better than he is!

Mom: Mike punched you in the arm because he is jealous?

Chris: He punched me when I showed him that I'm better than him at his own game.

Mom: Oh my goodness. That sounds like a real problem I'll need to deal with. Hold that thought. We'll come back to it, but it's helpful for me to start at the beginning. How was school today?

Chris: Fine.

Mom: Good day?

Chris: Yep.

Mom: Everything good with your teachers?

Chris: Yep.

Mom: With the kids?

Chris: Yep.

Mom: Great. So, how were you feeling when you got home from school?

Chris: I was happy. I finished all of my homework in school, so I was excited to play Xbox.

Mom: Sounds good so far.

Chris: Yeah, but when I went to play, Mike and Eddie were already playing something.

Mom: Were you upset when you saw them already playing?

Chris: No. I was actually happy because Mike was playing my favorite game, but I know that I'm better at it than he is, so I was excited to show him how to get to the next level.

Mom: Got it. So, school was good today, you were happy when you got home because you had already finished your homework, and you were feeling excited when you saw Eddie and Mike playing Xbox because you thought you could help them with the game.

Chris: Yep.

Mom: I think that's great that you wanted to help Mike get to the next level. Some kids might compete with their brother or brag about how good they are, but you actually wanted to help your brother do better in the game. I'm impressed, Chris!

Chris: Yeah. He's been trying for the last week, and I know he is frustrated. I figured it out last night, and so I want to show him how to do it.

Mom: That's a great idea. Tell me what happened when you first walked in the room.

Chris: I sat down and started to watch Mike and Eddie playing. We were all sort of laughing and joking and having a good time. I even brought up drinks for all of us.

Mom: That was a nice thing to do.

Chris: (Appears proud.) I know.

Mom: So, then what happened after you gave them their drinks?

Chris: I just watched Mike for a while and tried to give him some pointers, but he kept telling me to shut up so that he could concentrate.

Mom: Do you remember what you were thinking when he told you to shut up?

Chris: I thought he shouldn't tell me to shut up because I have really good information about the game, and if he listened to me, he'd be a better player.

Mom: So, you were thinking you had information that would benefit him. That makes sense. I wonder what he might have been thinking?

Chris: He said I was distracting him!

Mom:	Oh, so when you talk while he plays, he gets distracted. I can understand that. Did you give him the quiet he asked for?
Chris:	Yeah, for the most part.
Mom:	For the most part? What does that mean?
Chris:	I was mostly quiet, but I had to tell him a few things so that he didn't keep messing up.
Mom:	How did that go?
Chris:	Not very well because he threw a pillow at me and told me to shut up a few more times. But he was doing it wrong, and I needed to tell him!
Mom:	I see. How do you think Mike might have been feeling when he threw the pillow at you?
Chris:	Probably mad.
Mom:	Probably mad. Yeah, I think you might be right about that. Do you remember what you were thinking?
Chris:	I was thinking that he needed to listen to me because I know more than him, and I can help him get to the next level.
Mom:	Ahh, so you were thinking you wanted to help. That's really nice of you to want to do that. Did you think that Mike wanted your help?
Chris:	Not really. But he still needs it.

Mom: OK. So, let me make sure I have this correct so far. You walked into the room with drinks for your brothers, which is a really nice thing to do. You were watching Mike play and trying to give him tips, but he told you that your talking distracted him. Then, he told you to shut up a few times and threw a pillow at you. These things helped you realize that he was getting mad and that he probably did not want help. You were convinced that he needed help, though, so you kept talking anyway.

Chris: Yep.

Mom: Then what happened?

Chris: When his character died, he gave the controller to Eddie. I got mad because I had been waiting to play. But I knew that Eddie had been waiting too, so I didn't say anything. I just sat there and tried to help Eddie with his game.

Mom: That's great that you were so patient and considerate of Eddie. How did Eddie seem to like your help?

Chris: I don't think he liked it either. He told me to shut up too.

Mom: How did that make you feel?

Chris: Mad—like they were ganging up on me when they should have been thanking me for my help!

Mom: Did you stop talking?

Chris: Mostly.

Mom: Mostly?

Chris:	Yeah. I tried to be quiet, but there were a few times where I had to yell out "Stop!" or "Go right!" He just ignored me and did the opposite of what I told him.
Mom:	How do you think he might have been feeling when he did the opposite?
Chris:	I don't know. He was probably getting mad.
Mom:	Then what happened?
Chris:	I got tired of watching him mess up. He was about to die, so I grabbed the controller and rescued his character. I was about five seconds from getting him to the next level, but that's when he and Eddie both started yelling at me. It was so hard to concentrate on the game with their screaming!
Mom:	Their screaming made it hard for you to concentrate and get Mike's character to the next level.
Chris:	Yep. It was so loud that I accidentally got his character killed, and then Mike punched me in my arm. Look how red it still is!
Mom:	It really is red, honey. That must hurt. I am going to need to talk to Mike about this because I never want any of you resorting to violence when you are upset. Before I talk to him, though, let's you and me keep talking and see if we can figure out how to avoid something like this happening again in the future.
Chris:	I have an idea for that! We can just put the Xbox in my room. Since Mike is so bad at it and doesn't listen to how to play better, maybe he shouldn't be allowed to play anymore.

> **Step 3: Understand the problem—recognize that Chris's intentions (to play with his brothers) were good, but the way he went about approaching them (stealing Mike's game controller) was unwise.**

Mom: Well, that's one idea for how to handle things with Mike. Is it OK if I run a different idea by you?

Chris: Sure. Do you want to take the Xbox away from Eddie too?

Mom: Not exactly. I'm thinking about something that might help all of you have more fun playing video games and even get to higher levels.

Chris: Well, that would be good if you could make that happen.

Mom: Better yet, I think you can make it happen! To start sharing my idea, I'm just going to say back to you what I heard you tell me. Sometimes when you hear someone else talk about what happened, you realize new things.

Chris: OK.

Mom: So, you told me that today was a good day for you overall, and you were feeling pretty happy when you got home. Last night, you figured out how to get to the next level in a game on Xbox, and so when you saw Mike and Eddie playing, you were excited to show them the new moves. You thought the new information about the game could really help them. All good so far?

Chris: Yep. All good.

Mom: You were kind enough to bring your brothers drinks, which I am sure they appreciated, and then you sat down and watched

	Mike play. You were giving him little tips here and there while he played. You told me that you thought he needed the tips, but you also said that Mike told you that your talking distracted him from playing. Is that right?
Chris:	Yes.
Mom:	Thank you for going through this with me. You are being so focused. When you hear this part of the story—the part where you were trying to help Mike but he found your help distracting—does it make you realize anything?
Chris:	That he should be better at listening and not getting distracted.
Mom:	(Laughs.) It would be nice if all of us could do two things at once, but that's pretty hard to do. Does it make you realize anything else?
Chris:	(Pauses. Looks confused at first, then responds.) Maybe I shouldn't have talked while he was playing? Maybe the way I was trying to help him didn't end up being all that helpful?
Mom:	(Gently) That's a really smart thing for you to realize, Chris. I think you may be right. I think your heart was in the right place, and you were trying to help Mike get to the next level—and I'm really proud of you for that! When you boys work together, you are unstoppable! I think you are also right, though, when you say that your kind of help ended up not being very helpful. In fact, it distracted him and made him upset.
Chris:	That's not how I meant it!
Mom:	I realize that, honey. For years, I've been trying to get you, Mike, and Eddie to be kind and help each other out. Today, you did

that—you were trying to help him get to the next level on his video game. That's just the kind of thing that I want. The only problem was the kind of help you gave. Giving him tips while he was playing ended up distracting him.

Chris: I guess.

Mom: The good news is that I can help you figure out more helpful ways to help Mike. That's actually the easy part in all of this!

Chris: There's one more part of the story you are forgetting.

Mom: What's that?

Chris: I grabbed his controller, and he got really mad about that.

Mom: Right. Remind me—what were you hoping to have happen when you grabbed the controller?

Chris: I was trying to play for him since he wouldn't listen to me.

Mom: You were trying to help again…

Chris: But I did it in a way that didn't end up actually being helpful, since I accidentally killed his player. It was sort of his fault, though! He was screaming at me, and I couldn't concentrate.

Mom: He was making so much noise while you were playing that you got distracted.

Chris: Yeah! (Pauses.) I guess I know how he felt when I was talking during his game.

Mom: Right. Wow. I think you've really realized a lot here, Chris. I think you have a whole new understanding of how sometimes a good idea can go wrong. And maybe you understand a little bit more about why Mike was feeling so mad.

Chris: Yep.

Step 4: Teach Chris the new social skills he needs to be successful in future situations.

Mom: Now, we just need to talk about how to maybe keep this kind of thing from happening again the next time you play video games with someone else. Do you have any thoughts on how your help can be more helpful?

Chris: Well, one thing I could do is tell Mike to pause the game so that he can listen to my tips without getting distracted.

Mom: That's a great idea, Chris! Waiting until the game is paused before you talk will give you the chance to help your brother but in a way that doesn't mess up his focus and concentration. I think that's a great solution! Do you have any other ideas?

Chris: Maybe I could show him how to get to the next level when it's my turn to play instead of talking and distracting him when it's his turn?

Mom: Both of those are fantastic ideas, Chris! I think either one would work. Should we run some of your ideas by Mike and Eddie and see what they think might work?

Chris: That's a good plan. They may have other ideas.

Mom: They might. I'm proud of you for realizing that and wanting to hear their thoughts.

Chris: Do you think Mike is going to punch me again?

Mom: I'm going to deal with the punching part. Let's you and I talk to him about the video game part and see if we can make it so that no one is feeling angry anymore.

Chris: Sounds good. Thanks, Mom.

LSCI Skills in Practice

Not every child remembers to say thank you after a taxing emotional conversation. The rewarding thing about the New Tools approach in working with kids like Chris is that they tend to be genuinely grateful to adults who help them understand where their right intentions went wrong.

There are several key strategies that Chris's mother used that can be helpful across most New Tools situations. Let's revisit a few of them.

1. Affirmation

The mother abundantly affirmed Chris's good intentions and right behaviors, including his bringing his brothers drinks, his idea to help Mike get to the next level, and his good focus in talking to his mom about what happened. Without this level of support, a child like Chris would likely have stayed stuck in his anger and indignation he felt toward his brothers. The affirmations of his positive behaviors allowed him the courage to examine his own actions.

2. Taking Your Time

You may have noticed that this New Tools conversation was a bit more detailed than the others we have reviewed so far. Many adults find that the New Tools approach is easier than other LSCI interventions because the child is grateful for our help rather than actively resisting us; however, it is also important to note that children who lack the social skills they need to be successful also tend to benefit from having social insights explained to them in greater detail. In this situation, even though the mother likely realized early on in the conversation where Chris had gone wrong, she resisted spelling it out for him—which would likely have increased his resistance and feelings of embarrassment. Instead, she took her time and used questions, summarizing, and paraphrasing to help Chris come to his own helpful conclusion about where he went wrong. This feeling of "figuring it out" is a powerful experience for kids, and their "self-discovered" knowledge tends to last much longer than insights that are directly given to them by adults.

3. New Tools or Reality Check?

Throughout the interview, Chris clung tightly to the belief that Mike needed his help with the video game and that if Mike would only have listened, the problem wouldn't have happened. If you are reading this book in order and recently learned about the Reality Check intervention (Chapter 6), you may have noticed that Chris had tunnel vision on his perception of reality.

Would it have been appropriate, then, for the mother to use the Reality Check intervention in order to help Chris broaden his perspective and see Mike's point of view? Certainly. A Reality Check could have been helpful in this situation.

> Whenever a child feels heard and understood, you have done something very right!

However, based on the emotions Chris displayed during Step 1—the anger that quickly revealed itself as confusion over what went wrong—his mother determined that the most important issue at hand was Chris's misunderstanding of video game etiquette. Likewise, the most useful skill Chris could gain in the situation was how to help at the right time and in the right way.

If the mother had used a Reality Check intervention to teach Chris alternate ways of perceiving the situation, would she have been wrong? Certainly not. The wonderful thing about the LSCI approach is its flexibility and helpfulness across many situations. Whenever a child feels heard and understood, you have done something very right!

You don't have to wait for a New Tools–type problem to occur in your family in order to make use of this new skill. Consider these ideas for helping your young person develop greater awareness of social cues and adopt more positive social behaviors:

- Role-play challenging situations, such as making a new friend, joining kids already at play, celebrating a success, or starting a conversation. Kids of all ages can benefit greatly from rehearsing basic social skills with a safe and trustworthy adult.

- Make a game that challenges your child to figure out "right ways" and "wrong ways" to handle challenging situations. For example, present the following scenario, and then challenge your child to come up with one "wrong way" and at least two "right ways" to achieve his desired outcome.

> **Scenario:** *Sammy wants to get a grade of B or better on his math test.*
>
> 1. **"Right" way:** Sammy studies his math every night for 30 minutes.
>
> 2. **"Right" way:** Sammy asks his teacher for extra-credit work.
>
> 3. **"Wrong" way:** Sammy steals a copy of the test from his teacher's desk the day before the test so he can work out the correct answers ahead of time.
>
> Adults and kids can take turns generating "right" and "wrong" responses to relevant situations.

Preview of the Next Chapter

In the next chapter, we will examine situations in which kids seem to have little or no remorse for their misbehavior and/or enjoy justifying their unacceptable behavior.

CHAPTER 8

THE ENCOURAGING EMPATHY INTERVENTION
Confronting Unacceptable Behavior

Keesha is in a fight with her friend Stacy. Keesha posts an embarrassing photo of Stacy on social media with a caption that reads "Slutty Stacy." Stacy is humiliated in front of her whole grade. When Stacy confronts Keesha about posting the photo, Keesha says, "What? Can't you take a joke? I didn't think you'd be so sensitive!"

Some young people have an uncanny ability to turn any problem situation into an opportunity to justify their behavior. In a one-two punch, Keesha first cyberbullied Stacy and then blamed Stacy for being too sensitive and not having a good enough sense of humor. Modern technology provided the perfect medium for Keesha's passive-aggressive behavior. She could hurt her friend without the natural deterrent of having to look her in the eye while doing so. Free from guilt, Keesha could trick herself into believing that the humiliation of her friend was justifiable.

The *Encouraging Empathy* intervention is designed to help young people who are comfortable with their hurtful behavior and who try to justify their misdoings through an endless series of excuses, rationalizations, or flat-out denial. These children create a uniquely difficult position for themselves. They act out in ways that alienate adults and yet need adult support desperately if there is to be real hope of positive behavioral change.

The Encouraging Empathy approach is invaluable because it gives parents and caregivers a framework to systematically confront their children's hurtful behavior (a neocortex function) without getting caught up in anger or outrage (a limbic system response) at their children's disturbing behavioral justifications. As challenging as this intervention may be to those who dislike confrontation, it is equally rewarding in its effectiveness as a tool to help young people change troubling and cruel behaviors.

Justification of Unacceptable Behavior

Justifying unacceptable behavior is a common self-defeating pattern of behavior. Young people caught up in this pattern tend to have good verbal skills and a history of successfully talking their way out of trouble by using variations on a few common justifications (Long, Wood, & Fecser, 2001), such as:

Basic Justification 1: "She started it."

Emily tells her little sister, Maggie, to stop singing because it is annoying. Maggie continues to sing. Emily tells Maggie a second time that if she doesn't stop singing, she is going to hit her. Maggie still continues to sing. Emily punches her little sister in the arm. Maggie begins to cry and tells their mother what Emily did. Emily responds by insisting, "She started it by singing that annoying song. I told her to stop. She knew it was coming. It's her own fault."

Basic Justification 2: "It's no big deal."

Timmy is caught stealing several bicycles from around his neighborhood. When questioned by the police, Timmy says he only took bikes that were not locked up. He never broke any chains or took bikes from inside anyone's house. Therefore, Timmy insists that what he did was not illegal.

Basic Justification 3: "No one would have done anything."

Silas and his sister are in the bathroom, arguing about whose turn it is to clean the shower. When her back is turned, Silas quickly leaves the room and holds the door closed so that she can't get out. When she yells at him to stop holding the door, Silas says, "I'll let you out after you clean the shower. If you don't clean it, you can stay in there all day!" His sister relents and does the chore, but when Silas lets her out, she immediately tells their father what happened. When summoned by their dad, Silas tells the truth about what he did, explaining, "You never make her do anything, so I made her do her chore today."

The 4-Step Process at Work in an Encouraging Empathy Situation

Parents and caregivers can feel especially frustrated by interactions with kids like Keesha, Emily, Timmy, and Silas due to the kids' lack of remorse coupled with sophisticated verbal skills to defend their behaviors. LSCI's 4-step process offers a highly effective way to avoid getting derailed by frustration and to stay focused on confronting the unacceptable behavior. All the while, the process is carried out with the level of respect necessary to bring about long-term changes in young people's outlooks and behaviors. Read on to learn how the 4-step process can guide you to more effectively confront your children's justifications while teaching them better ways to behave.

Step 1: Use the process of Drain Off to help Keesha reduce the intensity of her emotion.

- Unlike the other situations we have talked about so far, in Encouraging Empathy patterns, there is usually minimal emotion to drain off. You will see in the example below that Keesha feels very comfortable with her behavior toward Stacy and shows it through her calm, cool, confident attitude when her father first asks her what happened.

- On the other hand, parents may feel themselves becoming emotional in the early steps of this intervention because their child's steady stream of excuses and justifications creates feelings of anger and outrage.

- Parents must be ever cautious to maintain their composure as they begin to engage their child in a dialog about what happened.

Step 2: Use the Timeline to help Keesha put language to emotion.

- The Timeline stage will likely also seem fairly straightforward in an Encouraging Empathy situation because emotions are not clouding the child's recollection and retelling of events. Comfortable with her behaviors, Keesha does not lie or conceal the fact that she posted the photo and that Stacy was humiliated.

- Nonetheless, parents are encouraged to take their time during Step 2 and use the Conflict Cycle to get their children to talk about their perceptions, thoughts, feelings, and behaviors related to the problem situation. It is during this step that parents hear the justifications and rationalizations that are helping their children feel comfortable about their cruel behavior. It is only by nonjudgmentally gathering this information during Step 2 that parents can later effectively confront and help change a child's pattern of justifying unacceptable behavior.

- In Step 2, parents and caregivers should be on the alert for the three basic justifications listed above as well as these other typical ways of excusing their cruel behavior:

    o **Minimization:** I was just joking. I didn't know she would be so sensitive.

    o **Rationalization:** She gave me the photo. If she didn't want me to show it to people, she shouldn't have posed for it in the first place.

    o **Projection:** I didn't do anything wrong. She's just embarrassed, and so she's trying to get me in trouble.

    o **"Should" statements:** She should have been [OK with me posting her joke]. She should be able to take a joke.

Step 3: Understand the problem—recognize that Keesha is using excuses to justify unacceptable behavior. Confront the justifications and the behavior directly.

- If you anticipate that you will find it challenging to directly confront your child's justifications during this intervention process, you are not alone. Many people spend a lifetime avoiding confrontation. The problem is, verbally savvy kids know this. What's more, they count on the fact that they have out-talked adults before and will be able to do it again. Although it's normal for you to feel uncomfortable in a conflict situation, be assured that the Encouraging Empathy approach is not an in-your-face, make-them-admit-what-they-did approach. Far from it! Step 3 is all about a calm, rational, systematic confrontation of children's justifications. Simultaneously, it is a caring approach that lets them know they are supported even if their behavior is not.

- Tone of voice and body language are critical factors when it comes to the "benign" confrontation needed for this step. To be effective, the adult's tone should be calm, composed, and nonthreatening. Words should be direct and to the point. Body language should be nonthreatening. Respect should be communicated at all times.

Step 4: Teach Keesha needed skills for how to resolve a peer conflict assertively and respectfully.

- Many kids who justify unacceptable behavior do so as a choice. It's not that they lack skills to express anger or resolve conflict but rather that they find it rewarding to control situations, get their needs met (even at others' expense), and outwit adults.

- If the situation warrants it, parents are encouraged to use Step 4 to teach their children new skills for behaving better. It is possible that Keesha could benefit from learning how to resolve a conflict with a friend directly and respectfully.

- In other situations, it will be most effective for parents to simply but matter-of-factly remind their children that cruel behavior is never justifiable and that anytime it occurs, it will be addressed.

- For kids who have a pattern of justifying unacceptable behavior, knowing that an adult can see through their rationalizations and is willing to respectfully confront their excuses is a strong deterrent to continuing the unacceptable behavior.

The 4-Step Framework With Keesha and Her Father

In the pages that follow, we offer you an example of what an LSCI Encouraging Empathy intervention between Keesha and her father could sound like using the 4-step process. Remember that there is no "script" to an LSCI intervention. Your conversation with your child does not have to sound precisely like our example. We encourage you to learn from the structure and the key phrases we use but to always maintain your own authenticity in your interactions with a young person.

Step 1: Use the process of Drain Off to help Keesha reduce the intensity of her emotion, as needed.

Father: Keesha, I just got a text from Stacy's mother asking if she can call me tonight to discuss what's going on between you girls. What do I need to know before I talk to her?

Keesha: (Smirks.) She texted you? WTF? Stacy is so oversensitive. She's blowing this whole thing out of proportion.

Father: What whole thing?

Keesha: It's totally not a big deal. Just a picture on social media that she gave me, and now she's embarrassed about it. So ridiculous.

Father: She's upset because she gave you a picture, and now she's embarrassed about it?

Keesha: I guess. It was all just a big joke. I seriously didn't do anything wrong. She's just feeling dumb, and so now she's trying to get me in trouble.

Step 2: Use the Timeline to help Keesha put language to emotion.

Father: Tell me a little bit more about this photo. What do I need to know about it before I talk to Stacy's mom?

Keesha: It's nothing. It's just a picture of Stacy making pouty lips. She's the one who texted it to me.

Father: I've seen you girls taking those pictures of each other and taking selfies. What's got Stacy feeling embarrassed about this one?

Keesha: I guess she's mad because I posted it on social media as a joke, and a few kids ended up teasing her about it. It's not my fault that they talked sh*t about her!

Father: Ahh. So that makes a little more sense. You posted a photo of Stacy that she sent you, and some other kids made fun of her for it.

Keesha: Yeah, but it was just a joke. How was I supposed to know they'd make fun of her? Her mom should be talking to those kids' parents, not wasting your time.

Father: Well, I appreciate your concern for my time, but I never mind talking to one of your friends' parents or helping with a situation. I feel badly if kids are making fun of Stacy and she's feeling embarrassed. That's a really hard position for her to be in, don't you think?

Keesha: Not really. I just don't think it's a big deal.

Father: I get that from your reaction. I'd like to see the post before I talk to Stacy's mom so that I can see what the other kids have been posting about her.

Keesha: OK. I'll show you later after I finish my homework.

Father: I'd like to see it now. Stacy's mom is going to call me in about 15 minutes.

Keesha: (Tosses her phone to her father.) Fine. Go ahead.

Father: (Fiddles with phone.) I need your password to get in.

Keesha: Dad, can we just do this later? I have a lot of homework.

Father: (Sensing his daughter's first bit of discomfort in the conversation.) I need to see it now, honey. Is something wrong?

Keesha: No. I'm just busy, and this is such a waste of our time.

Father: I realize this seems silly to you. I'll just take a quick look at the post so that I can tell Stacy's mom that I saw it. Sound good?

Keesha: Fine. Here. (Keesha enters password and pulls up the social media posting for her dad.)

Father: (Points.) Is this the one? The one that is captioned "Slutty Stacy?"

Keesha: Yeah. I just added that because she's always saying that about herself. It's just a joke she and I always make.

Father:	So, "Slutty Stacy" is like a private joke between you and Stacy?
Keesha:	Yeah. She made it up.
Father:	She made it up. OK. So, she was OK with you posting her joke on her photo?
Keesha:	She should have been.
Father:	You think she should have been. But did she tell you ahead of time that it was OK?
Keesha:	No. That would be dumb, Dad. No one talks about things like that before we post stuff.
Father:	Got it. So, "Slutty Stacy" was a private joke between the two of you, and now it's a joke that lots of other kids know about.
Keesha:	Exactly. No big deal. It was always funny before, but now she's freaking out and acting like I did it on purpose just to make fun of her. How was I supposed to know that kids would post rude stuff about her? And isn't it her fault for taking a photo like that in the first place? I mean, seriously.
Father:	You think that Stacy should have known better than to take a photo like that.
Keesha:	Don't you?
Father:	(Laughs.) Well, if it was up to me, selfies wouldn't even exist, and neither would social media, so I can't really say whether or not Stacy should have taken the photo. Let me just see if I have this all right so I'm ready to talk to Stacy's mom in a few minutes. So, you say that Stacy texted you a photo of her making pouty lips, right? When did she send you the photo?

Keesha: A few weeks ago.

Father: Oh, a few weeks ago. OK. I didn't get that before. So, what made you post it last night?

Keesha: I don't know. Stacy has been sitting with other people at lunch this week, and she won't tell me why. I guess I posted the photo so that she would have to talk to me again.

Father: Oh, so you and Stacy have been in a fight?

Keesha: I wouldn't say a fight. I would just say that she had been ignoring me. (Smirks again.) We might be in a fight now, though.

Father: You think posting the photo with the caption "Slutty Stacy" might have turned this into a fight?

Keesha: Maybe—but only because she is totally overreacting.

Father: Got it. OK. So, Stacy texted you the photo a few weeks ago, and you just posted it online, along with the words "Slutty Stacy," which you say is a private joke between you and Stacy.

Keesha: That she made up.

Father: Right. That she made up. And now some kids have posted this really nasty stuff here. (Father scrolls through the comments section.)

Keesha: Yeah. Some of it's pretty crazy, right?

Father:	Some of it is really disgusting and rude. I would be horrified if kids posted things like this about you. I think I might know why Stacy's mom wants to talk to me.
Keesha:	I just hope she tells her daughter not to take photos like that anymore. She probably shouldn't make up those kinds of nicknames for herself either.
Father:	I agree with you about both of those things. Is there anything else I need to know about this before I talk to Stacy's mom?
Keesha:	Not really.

Step 3: Understand the problem—recognize that Keesha is using excuses to justify unacceptable behavior. Confront the justifications and the behavior directly.

Father:	OK. Thank you, Keesha, for taking the time to tell me about what happened with Stacy today. Stacy started sitting with other kids at lunch and wouldn't talk to you about why she changed her seat. I can definitely understand why you were feeling upset. It's really hard to feel ignored, especially when it's by a close friend and you have no explanation as to the reason for it.
Keesha	Exactly.
Father:	There are a few things I don't understand as well, though, Keesha. You told me that the photo you texted was "just a joke," but I can't help but wonder what would be funny about posting a photo with the caption "Slutty Stacy."
Keesha:	I told you, it's a joke she and I always make. She made it up!
Father:	Yes, you did tell me that, and I believe that when she made it up

about herself that the two of you thought it was funny. Here's the thing. Private jokes are just that—private. They are funny because a small group of people have a special kind of understanding. When private jokes are spread to others without an explanation of the joke, they can be misinterpreted and misunderstood.

Keesha: That's not my fault.

Father: We are all responsible for the words we use and the things we choose to post online, Keesha. Jokes should make people laugh and feel good. I think a part of you knew that posting that photo with that caption would make Stacy feel bad instead of good. Embarrassing someone in this way is never funny. It is cruel, and it is unacceptable.

Keesha: Well, it's not my fault that other people posted nasty comments online. That's on them. Stacy shouldn't be blaming me for it.

Father: I agree that the people who posted those disgusting comments are responsible for their own actions, Keesha. No doubt about that. I also believe that without the photo being posted by you in the first place, those comments would not have been made, and the private joke you had with Stacy would not be out there for the public to use against her. You have responsibility for the consequences of your actions—even the consequences that you did not directly control. I'm asking you to think about that.

Keesha: (Silently crosses her arms over her chest. After an extended silence, speaks quickly.) It was just a stupid joke. You are overreacting just like Stacy did. Everyone always blames me for things. It's so unfair.

Father: I appreciate you sharing your perspective with me, Keesha. It is just a thought for you to consider.

Step 4: Teach Keesha needed skills for how to resolve a peer conflict assertively and respectfully.

For the benefit of demonstration, we are going to presume that Keesha did post the photo with cruel intentions but did so due to a lack of knowledge of respectful ways to manage the conflict situation with her friend. As such, her father uses Step 4 to offer his daughter new strategies for resolving a fight with a friend.

Father: (Allows a few moments of silence after his previous statement.)

Keesha: Can I go start my homework now?

Father: Yes, sweetheart. I know you said you had a lot of homework to get done tonight. I just need three more minutes of your time, and I think we can bring an end to this conversation for now. Can you give me three more minutes?

Keesha: (Arms crossed) Fine.

Father: Thank you. As you are well aware, I've never been a teenage girl myself, but I do remember watching my sisters get in all kinds of arguments with their friends when we were in school. They'd come home and be so upset about things that had happened, and I remember lots of times when your Aunt Lori would dwell on her anger and plan how to get revenge on other kids.
The thing is, she lost a lot of really good friendships because he was always so determined to hurt anyone who had hurt her.

Keesha: So?

Father: So, I don't want to see you getting stuck in that same pattern. I know it might feel good to get back at someone in the moment, but in the long run, it feels a lot better to feel good about yourself as a person and be proud of how you treated others.

Keesha: So, am I supposed to let Stacy just stop talking to me and not do anything about it?

Father: No. I wouldn't say that doing nothing is very helpful either. Can you think of any ways you've made up with friends after fights in the past?

Keesha: Not really. Usually if I have a fight with someone, they're not my friend anymore.

Father: That's what I'd like to help you avoid. Some friendships are worth keeping, you know? You and Stacy have been friends for a long time. I have no idea why she stopped sitting with you at lunch this week, but I think it's worth a try to find out. Don't you?

Keesha: I tried to text her, but she didn't respond.

Father: What would you think about trying again? I can think of all kinds of times when I didn't notice a text because I had a whole bunch of messages coming in at once. Or times when I thought I responded but I didn't. There was even one time when your mom got really mad at me for not responding to one of her texts. It turned out that I did respond right away, but then I accidentally forgot to press "Send," and the text just sat on my phone for hours before she finally called me. She was so mad! Is it possible that something like that could have happened with Stacy?

Keesha: Well, no matter what, she should still be able to take a joke.

Father: (Ignores Keesha's bait to justify her behavior and sidestep his point.) Can we agree that when you are feeling ignored by a friend in the future, you will talk to them face-to-face and figure out exactly what the problem is instead of assuming the worst and doing something to get back at them?

Keesha:	I guess.
Father:	Do you have any other ideas for how to handle being ignored?
Keesha:	I can just hang out with my other friends for a while.
Father:	That's a great idea too. Sometimes we all just need a little bit of space, right?
Keesha:	I guess.
Father:	Thanks for sticking around for the extra few minutes. I think you know where you went wrong and understand that posting photos of others without their permission is never OK. I am going to call Stacy's mom now, but I think we have a good, solid plan that I can share with her. Is there anything else you want to add for now?
Keesha:	You can tell Stacy's mom that I'm sorry about posting the picture. I'll apologize to Stacy tomorrow at school.
Father:	Great idea. I'm proud of you for being willing to talk this through.

Benign Confrontation is an LSCI strategy used to shed light on the flaws in a young person's justifications for unacceptable behavior while still maintaining a caring relationship with her.

LSCI Skills in Practice

Benign Confrontation is an LSCI strategy used to shed light on the flaws in a young person's justifications for unacceptable behavior while still maintaining a caring relationship with her. This is a process that requires adults to:

Step 1: Control feelings of anger or outrage that may be inspired by the young person's apparent lack of remorse.

Step 2: Listen to the child's story and note the justifications she uses to excuse her cruel behavior.

Step 3: Be willing to directly confront the justifications in a nonthreatening but firm way.

Step 4: Use their positive relationship with the child to offer better ways to cope with thoughts and feelings in future stressful situations.

Here are highlights of how Keesha's father carried out the strategy of Benign Confrontation in this situation:

1. Whenever we receive a call from our child's teacher or another parent, it is natural for us to become either immediately defensive of our child or suddenly suspicious of her guilt. In this situation, Keesha's father did neither. Rather, **he effectively controlled any strong emotional reactions, which enabled him to calmly and logically gather the facts of what happened.** Notice how in Step 1 he remained emotionally neutral as he invited Keesha to have a conversation.

2. Though Keesha's retelling of events was fairly straightforward, her father took his time to carefully gather the facts from his daughter's point of view. He did so without judgment or interjection, which helped Keesha feel secure enough to continue the dialog. Using careful listening skills, the father noted the justifications his daughter used, such as:

- It was no big deal.
- It was just a joke.
- It was always funny before, but now she's freaking out…
- How was I supposed to know that kids would post rude stuff about her?
- Isn't it her fault for taking a photo like that in the first place?
- She is totally overreacting.
- She is the one who made up the nickname.

3. In Step 3, the father systematically returned the conversation to examine several of the justifications Keesha used earlier in the conversation. For example:

- In response to Keesha justifying posting the photo as "just a joke," the father benignly confronted her excuse by saying, "I can't help but wonder what would be funny about posting a photo with the caption 'Slutty Stacy.'"

- He also confronted her rationalization about sharing the private joke with others through the social media posting, saying, "Here's the thing: Private jokes are just that—private. They are funny because a small group of people have a special kind of understanding. When private jokes are spread to others without an explanation of the joke, they can be misinterpreted and misunderstood."

- The father benignly confronts Keesha's justification that it's not her fault that people posted cruel comments about Stacy by pointing out: "I agree that the people who posted those disgusting comments are responsible for their own actions, Keesha. No doubt about that! I also believe that without the photo being posted by you in the first place, those comments would not have been made, and the private joke you had with Stacy would not be out there for the public to use against her."

4. At the end of Step 3, Keesha started to show signs of defensiveness due to her father's persistent but benign verbal counters of her justifications. ("It

was just a stupid joke. You are overreacting just like Stacy did. Everyone always blames me for things. It's so unfair.")

This is a true turning point. This is the moment where Keesha begins to experience some discomfort with her behavior—which is a main goal of the Encouraging Empathy intervention. We want kids who usually feel no remorse for cruel behavior to begin to realize that perhaps their behavior is unacceptable.

Note that when Keesha's father picks up on her change in tone, he skillfully takes a small step back. Rather than giving in to the temptation of driving home his point, the father wisely avoids creating this kind of win–lose dynamic between him and his daughter. Instead, he understands a young person's need to save face and allows her this relationship-enhancing dignity by simply saying, "It was just a thought for you to consider."

Time is on our side in parenthood. When we have a strong relationship with our kids—based on dignity and respect—we don't need to rush all of the learning moments into a single conversation. Because it is clear that Keesha has had a change in the way she is thinking, the father knows that he can reinforce the point again at a later time rather than risking the gains he made in the conversation.

Bright, intuitive kids often take pleasure in being able to outmaneuver their peers and parents through the use of seemingly plausible explanations for self-serving behavior. The situation between Keesha and her dad is a great example of how a parent or caregiver can be extremely effective in confronting justifications for unacceptable behavior and teaching kids greater accountability for their behaviors. Seize the opportunity to practice the skill of benign confrontation anytime you hear your child justifying unacceptable behavior:

- TV shows and movies often celebrate intelligent characters who are able to manipulate others and justify their behaviors. Parents can use these "dramatized'" depictions as nonthreatening ways to talk with their kids about short-term gain versus long-term impact on a person's relationships, personal freedoms, etc.

- Be aware that the instant gratification of revenge or manipulation is intensely appealing to many young people. A parent's challenge is to help their children find ways to get their needs met that are both satisfying and constructive.

Preview of the Next Chapter

In the next chapter, we will examine situations in which kids act out impulsively and then feel intense guilt and shame.

CHAPTER 9

THE STRENGTHENING SELF-CONTROL INTERVENTION
Helping Kids Overcome Impulsivity and Guilt

Lisa is hanging out with some friends after school. Riya pulls out a cigarette and asks Lisa if she wants to smoke. Lisa knows she is not allowed to smoke and turns Riya down twice before giving in to the pressure of her friends. Later, Lisa's mother smells the cigarette smoke and asks Lisa about it. Lisa lies to her mother and denies having smoked. When Lisa's mother finds a cigarette butt right outside of Lisa's window, she is angry. She confronts her daughter, asking, "If you weren't smoking, why is there a cigarette out here with your lip gloss on it?"

At first, Lisa gets angry and calls her mother a "nosy bitch." Soon after, though, she feels guilty for having smoked, lied, and cursed at her mother. Lisa finds her mother, admits to having smoked, and tells her mother she should be grounded for six months. Lisa begins to cry and cannot look her mother in the eye because she is feeling so overwhelmed with guilt and shame.

If you are reading the chapters of this book in order, you will immediately note the contrast between this situation and the previous one. Whereas the Encouraging Empathy intervention is used with young people who feel little remorse about their unacceptable behavior, the *Strengthening Self-Control* interventon is designed to help young people who act out impulsively and then feel burdened by intense feelings of guilt and shame. The goal of this LSCI intervention is to strengthen a young person's self-control and self-confidence by building her awareness of her positive qualities.

> The goal of this LSCI intervention is to strengthen a young person's self-control and self-confidence by building her awareness of her positive qualities.

Strengthening Self-Control

As noted in Chapter 4, self-regulation is a term used to describe a person's ability to control emotions and resist impulsive behaviors. Kids rely on self-regulation skills at home, in school, and in their interactions with others. Certain diagnostic conditions, such as ADHD, mood disorders, and sensory processing issues, along with traumatic life experiences, such as abuse and neglect, can make self-regulation especially challenging for children.

> *Self-regulation* is a term used to describe a person's ability to control emotions and resist impulsive behaviors.

The Strengthening Self-Control intervention is especially helpful for kids who struggle with self-regulation and have a pattern of acting on impulse and then experiencing deep regret. This regret often shows up in the form of self-loathing statements such as the following:

- *I hate myself.*
- *I'm the worst kid in the world.*
- *I'm such a loser.*
- *I can't control myself.*
- *I deserve to be punished.*
- *It would have been better if I were never even born.*

Many of these kids feel guilt and remorse so intense that they are driven to seek punishment.

The parent's or caregiver's goal in a Strengthening Self-Control situation is twofold:

1. First, the adult aims to relieve some of the overwhelming feelings of sadness, guilt, shame, remorse, and regret from the child's shoulders through

emotional support and the use of abundant affirmation. To this end, parents highlight the child's positive qualities, acknowledge good choices she made, and point out where self-control was shown.

2. Second, the adult assists the young person in recognizing that mistakes are a part of being human, poor decisions are made by everyone from time to time, and each day offers a new opportunity to improve.

The 4-Step Process at Work in a Strengthening Self-Control Situation

Whereas Encouraging Empathy situations often inspire feelings of anger and outrage in an adult, Strengthening Self-Control incidents are likely to cause an adult to begin to feel some of the same despair and hopelessness kids like Lisa experience in the aftermath of a misbehavior. As caregivers, we must be aware of the impact that interactions with a distraught child can have on our amygdala, and we must work to remain centered in the problem-solving part of our brain in order to effectively help lift and support the young person.

Read on to learn how the 4-step LSCI process can guide you to help strengthen the self-control and self-confidence of a guilt-ridden young person.

Step 1: Use the process of Drain Off to help Lisa reduce the intensity of her emotion.

- The first clue you may be dealing with a Strengthening Self-Control situation is often found in the child's demeanor. Crying, hiding her eyes, withdrawing from others, and making self-loathing statements are all characteristic of a child who is overcome by feelings of guilt and shame. In these situations, a parent's or caregiver's goal is to bring the child to a place where she can talk about what is making her so very upset. Helpful Drain-Off phrases include:

- o I can see that you are feeling really upset right now. I don't know what has caused you to feel this way, but I am here to support you no matter what. I will help you figure this out.

- o I can tell you feel really badly about what happened. You are beating yourself up, wishing you would have made a better choice. That is what we are here to learn. We can work through this together.

- o Right now, you are feeling terrible about what happened with your sister. The way you feel is understandable. I think that, together, we can make this turn out OK.

- Sometimes, the clues that a child is feeling burdened by guilt and sadness are not as obvious. It is certain that some young people, when consumed by self-hatred, act out in aggressive ways. Calling her mother a "nosy bitch," for example, was not exactly Lisa's most endearing moment. Even when kids don't immediately reveal their painful feelings, Step 1 of this process helps parents and caregivers avoid misguided emotional responses to troubling surface behaviors. It keeps us on a relationship-building, problem-solving track by reminding us to drain off any type of intense emotion before trying to determine the heart of the issue.

Step 2: Use the Timeline to help Lisa put language to emotion.

- Once the young person's intense emotion (be it anger, sadness, guilt, or shame) is thoroughly drained off, the mother's job is to help Lisa put language to her emotions by asking Timeline questions that help her daughter talk about what happened and begin to make sense of the big picture of events. The Timeline steps help Lisa gain clarity on what actually happened versus what her guilt-ridden amygdala made her think happened.

- The Conflict Cycle is a helpful tool for separating actual facts from emotional recollections. As Lisa tells her story, her mother should listen carefully for moments in which Lisa showed self-control, made good decisions, acted in good faith, or demonstrated other positive qualities.

The mother should paraphrase these instances aloud to lay the groundwork for more thoroughly helping Lisa gain a new understanding of her problem in Step 3.

Step 3: Understand the problem—recognize that Lisa acted out impulsively and is now feeling intense guilt over her actions. Help Lisa understand that she has more self-control than she realizes.

- The LSCI process gives Lisa and her mother a roadmap for understanding Lisa's self-defeating pattern and bringing about long-term positive changes in self-regulation and in their parent–child relationship. Contrast these outcomes with what would likely have happened if Lisa's mother chose instead to use a strictly behavioral response when her daughter called her a "nosy bitch." Had a rote, reactive "behavior = punishment" model been used, it seems certain that Lisa's perception of herself as "the worst daughter ever" would have been reinforced. It also seems certain that Lisa's pattern of reverting to disrespectful, challenging behavior under stressful situations would repeat itself over and over again.

- Rather than going down this relationship-damaging, amygdala-driven road, Lisa's mother should use the information gathered during Steps 1 and 2 to bring her daughter to realize these new insights:

    o   Lisa has more self-control than she realized. Even under tempting circumstances and group pressures, she shows the capacity to control herself and make good choices.

    o   Lisa made a mistake, and that's OK. Mistakes are a part of being human and even offer an opportunity to learn new things. Mistakes do not mean that she is a terrible person or deserving of punishment.

- o   Lisa possesses many great qualities that will help her make good choices and learn from mistakes in the future.

- o   Lisa is loved and valued, no matter what.

Step 4: Teach Lisa skills for how to strengthen her self-control and self-confidence.

- A priority in Step 4 for parents and caregivers is to teach Lisa how to cope with stress so that:

  - o   She avoids acting out impulsively.

  - o   She can forgive herself when she makes a mistake rather than becoming overwhelmed by guilt and shame.

- Lisa would also benefit from learning that, in stressful situations, it can be extremely helpful to use calming strategies to help settle the emotional part of her brain and fully engage her thinking, logical brain. Step 4 is a great time to teach and practice a handful of calming strategies, including:

  - o   Taking 10 deep breaths
  - o   Movement—e.g., taking a short walk or pushing against a stable wall
  - o   Getting a drink of water
  - o   Imagining a peaceful place
  - o   Having a crunchy snack
  - o   Smelling a calming essential oil such as lavender
  - o   Squeezing a stress ball or hugging a special stuffed animal

- Lastly, Step 4 is the perfect time to teach kids that, during stressful moments, it is more important than ever to slow down, think about taking control of problems (instead of letting problems take control of them), talk to someone else about their feelings, and avoid acting out impulsively in ways that create new problems.

A Note on the Role of Punishment in Discipline

One of the most frequent questions we are asked by parents is, "Where does discipline fit in to the LSCI approach?" In this particular incident, Lisa's mother might understandably think, "If my kid smokes in the house and calls me a bitch, she needs to be punished!"

The most important question we pose in return is, *What is the purpose of discipline?* If, as we believe, the purpose of discipline is to teach children the skills they need to avoid repeating poor behavior, then we would answer with confidence that the LSCI approach is a disciplinary one through and through. When a young person actively participates in an LSCI conversation, is cooperative, and seems to have learned something, we believe discipline—in its most genuine form—has been carried out.

It is critical to note that there is a distinct difference between *discipline* and *punishment*. The brain systems involved with punishment are primitive, reactive, and amygdala-driven.

Relating to a challenging child on this kind of emotional level typically results in a mirrored, emotional response from the child. Far too often, it perpetuates a cycle of angry, reactive interactions.

Punishing children is quite different from disciplining them. Discipline relies on adults engaging the problem-solving part of their brain and making decisions based on helping kids understand their behavior better. Effective discipline has everything to do with adults controlling their emotions in the moment and making thoughtful decisions that help children strengthen their self-control in the long term.

The 4-Step Process With Lisa and Her Mother

Step 1: Use the process of Drain Off to help Lisa reduce the intensity of her emotion.

Lisa: (Crying) I'm sorry, Mom. I'm sorry. I'm just so sorry I said that. I don't know why I always do things like that.

Mother: (Approaches her daughter and puts her arm around her shoulders lovingly). I know you are sorry, honey.

Lisa: No, Mom, really. I am the worst daughter in the world. You didn't deserve that. All you did was ask me if I had been smoking, and I lied to you and called you a terrible name. I am so sorry. Please forgive me.

Mother: I can tell you feel really badly about what happened. I forgive you.

Lisa: I don't deserve to be forgiven. I deserve to be grounded for what I did. I do the dumbest stuff and say the meanest things when I get upset. I don't even know why I do it. I don't mean any of it. I hate myself when I get like this.

Mother: (Puts her other arm around Lisa to hug her). You are beating yourself up, Lisa. I know that you wish you hadn't said those things. I know that you don't mean the things you say when you are upset. I am here to help you figure out how to keep your temper under control.

Lisa: (Looks at her mother.) I don't think anyone can help me, Mom. I just keep doing this stuff over and over. I tell myself I won't let it happen again, but then it does. I'm hopeless.

Mother:	You are feeling hopeless right now, Lisa, but I am feeling hopeful. Just the fact that you are willing to sit with me and start to talk about things tells me that you are really trying to take more control. We are going to work through this together. It may take some time, and you might mess up again here and there, but I will always be here to help you.
Lisa:	(Sinks her head into her mother's shoulders).

Step 2: Use the Timeline to help Lisa talk about the sequence of events.

Mother:	Take your time, honey. It's OK to cry when you are upset. I know this has been a long day for you.
Lisa:	This day feels like it has been 30 hours long!
Mother:	Some days feel like that. How was school today?
Lisa:	Boring.
Mother:	Did anything bad happen at school?
Lisa:	We had a stupid math test.
Mother:	How do you think you did?
Lisa:	Fine. It was just boring.
Mother:	(Smiles.) OK. Well, I'm glad you think you did OK on it, and I'm glad it's over. Did anything else happen?

Lisa:	Not really.
Mother:	How are things going with your friends?
Lisa:	(Sighs). Ugh. Mom, I did not want to even smoke that cigarette, but Riya was so pushy about it. She kept making fun of me and insisting that you'd never even find out. I knew I'd get caught. I'm so dumb! (Becoming visibly upset again)
Mother:	You are feeling dumb for getting caught.
Lisa:	I'm feeling dumb for having let Riya push me around and make me do stuff I don't even want to do!
Mother:	Oh, got it. You're mad at yourself right now for letting Riya convince you to do something.
Lisa:	Exactly. I said no two times, but then the other girls started smoking too, and I didn't want to be the only one not doing it.
Mother:	Wow. You turned Riya down twice?
Lisa:	Yeah.
Mother:	That's impressive, honey! Resisting pressure from friends isn't easy at any age. I still feel like I get too easily talked into things by my friends, and I'm definitely old enough to know better. I'm really proud of you for showing enough confidence and control to have turned down Riya's offers twice.
Lisa:	Yeah, but I still gave in at the end, so there's really nothing to be proud of, is there?

Mother: I'm feeling proud of your efforts, Lisa, even if things eventually got off course.

Lisa: Thanks.

Mother: So, tell me what Riya said to you.

Lisa: First, she just handed me the pack of cigarettes and a lighter, and I said that I didn't feel like smoking and just handed them back. She didn't say anything, but then, like, five minutes later she took out a cigarette, lit it, and handed it to me. I pretended to take one puff, then handed it to Lila. Ten minutes later, Riya handed me the whole pack again and said she wasn't taking no for an answer from anyone. Everyone else took a cigarette, so I just took one too. I know it was a really stupid thing to do! You don't have to let me hang out with those guys anymore. I know you can't trust me to make good decisions after this.

Mother: Thank you for giving me all of that information. That actually tells me a few very important things—like the fact that you actually made two very smart decisions in saying no to the cigarettes the first time and then just pretending to smoke the second cigarette before you passed it on. It sounds to me like you were really using your head, which is something we have been working on. I'd say you showed some real progress today.

Lisa: But what about the fact that the third time I caved? And the fact that I lied to you? And called you a bad name? That's not progress! That is just more of me messing up!

Mother: You are working pretty hard to get me to focus on the bad stuff, aren't you? I have to admit that I prefer to focus on all of the times you got it right.

Lisa: Well, all I can think about is how nice you are being and how I don't even deserve it. I called you a nosy bitch, Mom! I cursed at you. I'm a terrible person.

Mother: Let's focus on that part since I can tell that it's still really troubling you. Do you remember what you were thinking after your friends left?

Lisa: I was running around my room spraying air freshener and terrified that you were going to find out that we had been smoking in the house.

Mother: OK. So, you were making an effort to get the situation back to normal and get things back under control. Do you remember how you were feeling?

Lisa: I was panicking! I could smell the smoke on my blanket, and I was trying to figure out how to wash it since air freshener wasn't cutting it.

Mother: It sounds like a really stressful situation!

Lisa: It was! Then you knocked on my door, and I was terrified. When you came in and asked if we had been smoking, I froze! I didn't know what to say. A part of me wanted to just admit it to you, but I had been working so hard to cover it all up that another part of me just took over and lied. I'm sorry!

Mother: OK. Well, thanks for being honest with me about what was going on in your head. I do know what it feels like to just have my brain freeze up when I'm stressed out. In between the first time I asked you about the smoking and the second time I came in your room when I had found the cigarette butts, do you remember what you were thinking then?

Lisa: Honestly, I barely even remember. I think I just got into my bed and was trying to figure out how to wash my blankets without you being suspicious! When you came back, I was so stressed out, I was about to cry. (Her speech starts to become very rapid.) Then I saw the cigarette butt in your hand, all of my stress just took over, and I yelled at you, and I know it was wrong, and I am so, so sorry about the whole entire thing, and I should be grounded!

Mother: I believe that you are sorry, honey. I forgive you for making that mistake. Try to take a few breaths. You're doing a really good job thinking this whole thing through, and I am not angry with you. I want to help you figure this whole thing out so that maybe we can stop it from happening again.

Lisa: Like I can ever stop messing up? Yeah, right.

Mother: You've already made a lot of good decisions today, and I believe that you have many more yet to come. Let's see if we can think about where to go from here. Do you mind if I just kind of go back through everything you've told me so far and make sure I have all of the details?

Lisa: Sure. Go ahead.

Mother: OK. So, things went OK at school today. After school, you were hanging out in your room with a couple of your friends when Riya had the idea to smoke. She handed you a pack and a lighter, but you handed it back without taking one. Is that right so far?

Lisa: Yeah. I also told her that you'd kill me if we smoked in the house, but she just lit her cigarette anyway.

Mother: What were you thinking when she did that?

Lisa: I was thinking that either you were going to kill me for letting her or she was going to hate me for stopping her.

Mother: That is a stressful position for you to be in.

Lisa: It was!

Mother: After you handed the cigarettes back the first time, Riya lit a second cigarette and gave it to you. You passed that cigarette on to Lily, but later on, Riya still insisted on everyone smoking.

Lisa: I think we were all tired of dealing with her at that point, and it was just easier to say yes!

Mother: I get that. So, all of you smoked, and then you threw the butts out the window.

Lisa: Yeah—that was a really dumb thing to do. I was going to go get them, but I got busy trying to air out my room.

Mother: Right. Then I came in and asked you about the smoke I thought I smelled. That made you panic a little. You froze up and denied smoking but then felt really bad. When I came back a few minutes later after finding the butts outside, you had gotten yourself more worked up. By the time I asked you about the smoking again, you lost control and called me a nosy bitch. As soon as those words came out of your mouth, though, you started to regret having said them. You've been feeling guilty and beating yourself up ever since. Did I leave out anything important?

Lisa: No. I think you got it all.

> **Step 3: Understand the problem**—recognize that Lisa acted out impulsively and is now feeling intense guilt over her actions. Help Lisa understand that she has more self-control than she realizes.

Mother: Wow. That's really a lot of detail. Thank you for helping me understand all that. You know, at the beginning of all this, it would have been easy for both of us to think this whole thing was just about me checking up on you and you reacting by calling me a name. But now that we've talked it through, I am realizing there is a whole lot more to the situation.

Lisa: (Confused) What do you mean?

Mother: When I realized you and your friends had been smoking in the house, I admit I was angry. I could feel my brain lighting up. Then, when you called me a nosy bitch, it felt like my brain was on fire for a few seconds. Believe me, I was ready to ground you for six months like you suggested. When I walked out of your room, that was me making a conscious decision to give myself a little break and to calm down and regain control of myself before I said anything that I would regret.

Lisa: I wish I could control myself before I did dumb things!

Mother: Here's the thing that I learned from our conversation, Lisa. You did control yourself today! Riya tried pretty hard to convince you to smoke, and you turned her down twice. You also tried to tell her not to smoke in the house. You have a lot more self-control than you are giving yourself credit for. You were in a very stressfu situation today, caught between your friends' wishes and my rules, and you made several good choices.

Lisa: But I gave in. I let them smoke, and I smoked too. I'm so stupid!

Mother:	After several tries, you let them smoke. That was something you wish you hadn't done. I am glad you realize that now. But giving in to pressure from friends doesn't make you stupid. It makes you a pretty typical teenager. You made a mistake, and that's OK. Mistakes are a part of being a kid. My job as a mom is to help keep you from making the same mistake again.
Lisa:	Good luck with that. I do a lot of dumb stuff.
Mother:	Welcome to the family. I do a lot of dumb stuff too, Lisa. And when it happens, I try to do what I did earlier today—calm myself down, then figure out the best way to make things right.
Lisa:	Well, that's really smart. I always end up making a mistake, then getting so upset that I make things even worse.
Mother:	Wait. Say that again.
Lisa:	I said that what you did was really smart. I always end up making a mistake, then getting so upset and making things even worse.
Mother:	That's a really great insight, Lisa. Just let that sink in for a minute. I think you are exactly right that when you start to get upset about a situation, your brain usually freezes up, and you start to panic. Once you panic, you sometimes say and do things that make a situation worse—like lying or calling me a name.
Lisa:	I hate that I do that!
Mother:	The good news is that, now that you realize that you have this pattern, you have the power to change it! You have control over your behaviors, Lisa. You are a really smart, kind, loving kid who makes good choices when you are feeling calm. You can learn ways to calm yourself down even in stressful situations like the one you were in today so that you can keep making the good choices.

Lisa: How? I feel like I can't control myself when I get upset. I feel like I become a whole different person.

Step 4: Teach Lisa skills for how to strengthen her self-control and self-confidence.

Mother: You know, you are not alone, Lisa. Feelings are really powerful. I don't think people give enough thought to how strong feelings—like the panic you had about getting in trouble for smoking in the house—can take over our brains and make us say and do things that are really out of character. I think a lot of people feel like they turn into a whole different person when they get upset. The thing is, once we realize this, we have the ability to think to ourselves, "Stop. I know what's happening here. This has happened to me before. I don't want to get out of control again, so I am going to give my brain the chance to calm down. I am going to take a few slow deep breaths. I am going to walk out of the room. I am going to get a drink of cold water. I am going to count to 20 before I say anything at all. I am going to choose whichever one of these strategies works best for me so that I can get back in control before I say or do something I will feel badly about later."

> "Stop. I know what's happening here. This has happened to me before. I don't want to get out of control again, so I am going to give my brain the chance to calm down."

Lisa: That taking deep breaths stuff never works for me.

Mother: I used to think that too. But that's because I was taking short, fast breaths instead of slow, deep ones. The kind of breathing that helps get your brain to feel calmer requires that you really slow things down—breathe in through your nose and out through your mouth. If you put your hand on your belly, you should be able to feel it filling up with air when you breathe in. Then, you push all of the breath out through your mouth.

Lisa: Mom, I can't do that when my friends are around. It'll look totally weird.

Mother: I get that. Maybe you can practice the deep breathing when your friends are not around. When you are with them and feel yourself getting stressed out, you can pick a different calming strategy that works better for you and is less obvious. Did any of the other options sound better?

Lisa: Maybe getting a drink of water. I think getting out of the room would help me have time to think and calm myself down. But what if they do something else when I am out of the room?

Mother: Well, that could happen, I guess. But at least you would have a calmer mind when you got back that could help you make a better decision.

Lisa: (Nods.)

Mother: The important thing is not so much which strategy you use to calm yourself down when you first feel yourself getting upset but that you use a strategy that works and stick with it until you feel calm and like yourself again. That way, you stay in control and can make the good choices that you usually make when you are not upset.

Lisa: OK. I'll try to figure out what works best.

Mother: Lisa, you are a great kid, and you make mistakes from time to time. Both of those things are true— it's not one or the other. All of us lose our tempers, and all of us are responsible for making things right after we mess up. That doesn't make us bad. It just makes us human. You are very loved, and I am grateful we had this conversation. I think we both learned a lot.

LSCI Skills in Practice

Self-regulation skills are a critical developmental skill for young people. For some, controlling thoughts and feelings seems to come as naturally as breathing, but for most kids (and many adults!), learning to control and manage emotions is a process. This process is every bit as deserving of step-by-step instruction from adults as any academic subject—and yet only rarely do we see this vital skill covered in school.

Parents and caregivers are the primary teachers of self-regulation in kids. The Strengthening Self-Control approach offers a structured way for young people to make the most of a problem situation by learning strategies for self-regulation.

There are several key strategies that Lisa's mother used to build her daughter's ability to self-regulate. These skills can be helpful across most Strengthening Self-Control situations and include:

1. Drain Off

Lisa was overcome by feelings of guilt and shame when the conversation first began. Although her emotions were "quieter" than some of the anger and rage you would typically see in an SOS or Reality Check situation, it is just as important to drain them off. Without doing so, Lisa would not be able to effectively engage the thinking, problem-solving part of her brain.

Note that even though the mother did drain off Lisa's feelings, some of them resurfaced later in the conversation. This is to be expected in any emotional conversation. Drain Off is not a once-and-done step but rather a continuous process of supporting and listening to young people.

When Lisa seems to be stuck in her guilt and self-loathing (*"Well, all I can think about is how nice you are being and how I don't even deserve it. I called you a nosy* bitch, Mom! I cursed at you. I'm a terrible person."), note that the mother made time to verbally acknowledge and address her feelings (*"Let's focus on that part since I can tell that it's still really troubling you."*) rather than just continuing on with her Timeline questions. It is only by attending to Lisa's pressing emotional concerns that her mother can help her move past them.

2. Abundant Affirmation

Had Lisa's mother followed her initial, amygdala-driven instincts and immediately punished Lisa for smoking in the house and cursing at her without having allowed Lisa to process the incident, Lisa's guilt and shame would surely have increased. Her negative beliefs about herself would have been confirmed, and the situation would have gone from bad to worse.

The neocortex-driven approach of using affirmation to acknowledge where Lisa went right—instead of harping on where she went wrong—allowed the mother to turn the tone of the conversation from heated to helpful. Sometimes in a problem situation, it can be difficult to find something to affirm. Many times, kids are pretty good at convincing us that what they did was all wrong (as you saw Lisa trying desperately to draw the conversation back to her mistakes and shortcomings). However, in order to be effective and turn the problem situation into a learning opportunity, parents must find ways to genuinely affirm the positive qualities within the child and/or the glimmers of good choices that were made. These are the "numb values" that can be brought back to life and cultivated if the adult is willing to look for them.

3. Highlighting the Self-Control

Throughout the conversation, Lisa refers to her awareness of her poor self-regulation. (*"I do the dumbest stuff and say the meanest things when I get upset. I don't even know why I do it. I don't mean any of it. I hate myself when I get like this."*) Notice how the mother consistently highlights the instances in which Lisa did show control and did make good choices. (*"You actually made two very smart decisions in saying no to the cigarettes the first time and then just pretending to smoke the second one before you passed it on. It sounds to me like you were really using your head, which is something we have been working on. I'd say you showed some real progress today."*) By emphasizing for Lisa that self-regulation skills already exist within her, she massages (awakens) her daughter's self-confidence and sense of self-control.

4. Careful Attention to Skill Building

Lastly, the mother made the most of Step 4 by using it as an opportunity to teach Lisa specific strategies for building even greater self-regulation. Talking, role playing, and practicing calming skills is one of the best ways parents and caregivers can help their kids avoid impulsive behavior during stressful times and thus prevent problem situations from occurring.

Instead of waiting for a Strengthening Self-Control problem situation to arise, there are preventive actions you can take if you live or work with a child who tends to act out impulsively and then becomes overwhelmed by guilt or sadness after the fact, including:

- Teach kids that, during stressful moments, it is more important than ever to slow down, think about taking control of problems (instead of letting problems take control of you), talk to someone else about how you are feeling, and avoid acting out impulsively in ways that create new problems.

- For younger kids, role playing how to behave during challenging situations can be particularly effective. Many kids can benefit greatly from rehearsing skills in decision making, resisting peer pressure, handling intense feelings, etc.

- Older kids may benefit from keeping a log of the daily challenges they face and the types of helpful solutions they can come up with. When kids practice slowing things down and thinking through helpful solutions before acting, they often gain an increased sense of control over their lives and a greater sense of personal power.

- For kids of all ages, it is helpful for parents to affirm the things their children do well. When children hear positive messages about themselves over time, they internalize the messages and change their own beliefs about themselves.

Preview of the Next Chapter

In the next chapter, we will examine situations in which kids become involved in self-defeating peer relationships.

CHAPTER 10

THE SET UP INTERVENTION
Resisting Manipulation in Sibling and Peer Relationships

Austin, the family's firstborn child, is a bright boy who gets along great with his friends but argues constantly with his younger siblings. In particular, Austin seems to take great pleasure in instigating conflicts with his volatile 11-year-old brother, Ricky. Today, when Ricky got up to use the bathroom, Austin changed the channel on the TV, then hid the remote control. When Ricky returned to the room to find his show changed, he—predictably—started to throw a fit. In searching for the remote, he shouted threats and curse words at Austin, threw pillows, overturned an ottoman, and knocked over a lamp. Ricky's upheaval in the family room led him to lose his TV privileges for one week.

Brothers are born, and parents have visions of how they will be best friends who always have each other's back. Sisters adore each other when they are little, and we imagine them side by side throughout life—each the other's biggest source of support.

And then, reality hits.

Sibling rivalry is the tale as old as time. A prominent issue for almost all families with more than one child, sibling rivalry is the competition, bickering, instigating, and envy between brothers and sisters. Although conflicts between siblings are a completely normal part of growing up, they can drive parents and caregivers crazy. In an already stressful outside world, adults may wonder, *"Why can't our family members just get along? Why do the kids have to be so awful to each other?"*

As siblings argue and push each other's buttons, parents often waver between quick intervention and "letting them work it out on their own." The truth is that siblings can be one another's greatest teachers when it comes to conflict resolution.

However, even though kids can clearly benefit from learning how to work through problems independently, it is also certain that siblings need a foundation of strategies and skills so they know how to do so fairly and effectively. Parents and caregivers are in the perfect position to guide their kids through the ups and downs of growing up together, helping them develop important life skills such as problem solving, sharing responsibilities, working together, empathy, compassion, and, in Ricky's case, avoiding "taking the bait" when set up by a sibling.

The Set Up

The final LSCI intervention we will look at in this book has everything to do with using the 4-step process to improve sibling* relationships. The *Set Up* intervention is designed to help young people better understand how their brothers or sisters may "set them up" to act out and how they can avoid being the unwitting victim of their siblings' manipulation.

A Set Up dynamic typically involves a bright, passive-aggressive sibling (may be older or younger) who enjoys pushing the buttons of an emotionally reactive brother or sister. In brain terms, one sibling is purposefully using his thinking brain to create an emotional brain reaction in his family member. This pattern repeats over and over again within the family because the reactive child doesn't realize he is being controlled—like a puppet on strings—by his clever and manipulative sibling. The parent's or caregiver's role in using the Set Up approach is to help the amygdala-driven child:

1. Gain awareness of how he is giving up his controls to others.
2. Develop new skills to resist others' manipulation.

You may be wondering what the Set Up approach, highly effective as a tool to help the emotional and reactive sibling, does to address the behavior of the purposefully manipulative brother or sister. Typically, the Encouraging Empathy approach (see Chapter 8) is the ideal way to confront the behavior of a "puppet master" sibling like Austin who finds satisfaction and pleasure in setting up emotionally reactive kids like Ricky.

> *In this chapter, we will describe the Set Up dynamic between siblings. Please note, however, that this intervention is equally applicable to peer relationships. Once kids understand the dynamics of resisting sibling manipulation, they simultaneously gain skills for avoiding manipulation by peers as well.

The 4-Step Process at Work in a Set Up Situation

The ultimate goal of the Set Up approach is to help kids learn skills to resist giving up control of their feelings and behaviors to others. Read on to learn how LSCI's 4-step process can guide you to support your emotionally reactive child while teaching him new skills to resist the manipulation of others.

Step 1: Use the process of Drain Off to help Ricky reduce the intensity of his emotion.

- The first priority in dealing with any emotionally reactive child is always to drain off his intense emotions. In Ricky's case, Drain Off will include getting Ricky to a safe space where his aggressive behavior stops and he can begin to talk about his feelings.

- Affirmation is an essential element of Step 1, and yet it can be very challenging for a parent or caregiver to even consider affirming a child who has been physically destructive. In situations like this, affirmation should not be abandoned; rather, the adult's task is to affirm things like the child's progress in calming down and his increasing willingness to talk to adults about what happened. Validation of the child's emotional state is also essential. Use phrases such as:

    o I can see that something has upset you terribly. I'd really like to know what it was so that I can try to help you.

    o You are feeling overwhelmed with anger right now. I can see you are working really hard to get yourself back under control.

- o It's so hard to control our feelings when they get this big. I appreciate how hard you are trying to calm down.

- It could be tempting for parents to react angrily to an outburst like Ricky's, but focused attention on his angry surface behaviors would be distractions from the central issue that motivated the behaviors in the first place—the fact that he was set up by Austin. To be effective, parents have to monitor their own emotions and take care to use their own self-soothing skills to avoid becoming caught in a relationship-damaging, situation-worsening Conflict Cycle.

Step 2: Use the Timeline to help Ricky put language to emotions.

- When Ricky's emotions are thoroughly drained off, it is time to begin using Timeline skills to gather information about Ricky's perceptions, thoughts, and feelings that led to his destructive behavior. Though Ricky will still likely be focused on finding the remote control and his parents will likely still be thinking about the mess in the family room, it is helpful for both to be willing to put their top-of-the-mind concerns to the side and to start at the beginning.

- As always, the Conflict Cycle is a very helpful guide in this step, allowing parents and kids to systematically and thoroughly consider all of the elements of the problem. As Ricky begins to connect Austin's actions with his own reactions, he will be well prepared for the insights still to come in Step 3. Without the "roadmap" provided by the Conflict Cycle, adults and kids become too easily derailed by emotional details.

Step 3: Understand the problem—recognize that Ricky was set up by his older brother, Austin.

- The goal of Step 3 is to help Ricky begin to understand how he was set up by Austin and how he gave up his emotional controls to his brother. Through the detailed information gathered in Step 2, the mother can use this step to help Ricky recognize the manipulation that took place.

- Through supportive questions and dialog, the mother will help Ricky understand that Austin purposefully hid the remote control because he knew it would cause Ricky to feel distressed and then to act out. This emotional manipulation is something Austin finds satisfying. Though it may be tempting for Austin to become the focal point of blame due to his intentionally cruel behavior, the key to an effective Set Up intervention is to keep the focus squarely on helping kids like Ricky realize they are accountable for their own behavior, no matter what. Even if someone else is provoking them, they must learn to stay in control of their own responses. The empowering part of the Set Up approach is helping emotionally reactive kids resist manipulation and increase self-control.

> **The empowering part of the Set Up approach is helping emotionally reactive kids resist manipulation and increase self-control.**

  o You may be wondering at this point if Austin's behavior should be addressed at all. The answer is a resounding yes—Austin's behavior must be confronted.

  o Timing is the issue. Austin's unacceptable behavior should be addressed after the mother has completed her Set Up conversation with Ricky and brought it to a satisfactory conclusion.

  o The conversation she should then have with Austin would likely be best handled by using the Encouraging Empathy approach to confront Austin's intentional cruelty toward his brother.

- One extremely helpful tool in the Set Up approach is the use of concrete analogies to teach kids about manipulation and control. In the example below, you will see how Ricky's mom likens Austin to a puppet master and Ricky to a marionette puppet to help Ricky understand how Austin's actions had a direct and predictable effect on Ricky's reactions. Other useful images you may want to use with kids in Step 3 of the Set Up intervention include:

- o   A match and a firecracker: In this situation, who was the match, and who was the firecracker? Who caused friction from behind the scenes, and who actually exploded and caused damage?

- o   A remote control and a television (especially relevant in this example)

- o   A lightbulb and a light switch

Step 4: Teach Ricky skills for how to avoid being set up and manipulated by others.

- Step 4 is a skill-building stage. Here, rather than punishing Ricky for allowing Austin to manipulate him, you have the opportunity to teach him the skills he needs to avoid giving up his emotional controls to others in future situations.

- In the dynamic that occurred in this situation, the learning Ricky needs can be further broken down into these subskills:

    - o   Skill 1: Learn to recognize and resist manipulation.

    - o   Skill 2: Learn to control anger (see Chapter 5 for anger control strategies discussed as part of the SOS intervention).

- Step 4 is completed when both the adult and child feel satisfied that the problem situation has been discussed, a new possible understanding of reality has emerged, and the young person feels better equipped with strategies to resist manipulation, whether it comes from a sibling, a peer, or even an adult.

The 4-Step Process With Ricky and His Mother

Mother: Ricky, I need you to come with me. Let's get out of the family room for a minute and into a space away from everyone else so that we can have some quiet.

Ricky: No! I'm staying right here. I'm not leaving until I can find the remote control. I know it's here. I know Austin hid it from me. He always does this to me. I hate him!

Mother: I know you are very upset about not knowing where the remote is. I promise you, I will help you find it. I'd just like to have a chance for us to talk first. I think it might be easier to find the remote when we are both feeling a little calmer.

Ricky: I can't calm down until I find it!

Mother: I'm worried that not being able to find it is what is making you so upset in the first place. Sometimes it helps to just get away from a problem for a while to let our brains settle. When we're calm, it's so much easier to think clearly about where lost items could be. I promise you that, after we talk, I will look for the remote with you before we do anything else.

Ricky: Fine! But Austin is not allowed to be in the family room either then. He'll just hide it again.

Mother: That's not a problem. Dad already told Austin that he needs to wait for me in his room. Let's you and I sit in the kitchen and talk. I'll be able to see him if he walks out.

Ricky: Fine. (Crosses arms and walks ahead of his mother, toward kitchen.
Sits down at table.)

Mother: (Sits next to Ricky at the round kitchen table.) It's so hard to control our feelings when they get this big. I appreciate how hard you are trying to calm down.

Ricky: (Takes a deep breath. Makes eye contact with his mother. Begins to cry softly.)

Mother: I can see that something has upset you terribly. I'd really like to know what it was so that I can try to help you.

Step 2: Use the Timeline to help Ricky put language to emotions.

Ricky: I just need to find the remote control.

Mother: (Gently) You are this upset because the remote control is lost?

Ricky: No. I am this upset because I have been waiting all day to watch my show, and now I can't watch it because I don't have the remote. Actually, I can't even watch it for a whole week now because Dad said I lost all of my TV privileges!

Mother: You were waiting all day to watch your show but couldn't find the remote?

Ricky: Well, I was watching TV but I got up to use the bathroom. When I got back, Austin had the remote and he had changed the channel. I asked him to give the remote back, but he just sat there laughing and saying he didn't have it. I know he knows where it is because he was laughing at me and saying "hot" and "cold" when I was walking around the room trying to find it. I told him I didn't have time for his games because my show was starting, but he just said, "Too bad," and kept laughing at me. I hate him!

Mother: So, you had the remote in your hand, you put it down when you

	went to the bathroom, and when you came back, the channel was changed and the remote was not where you put it?
Ricky:	Exactly. And I knew right away that Austin hid it because he does that to me all of the time!
Mother:	Yes, I have seen Austin do that to you before. I think you are probably right.
Ricky:	I know I'm right. He always does this to me. This whole thing is his fault.
Mother:	Tell me how we got from Austin making you play the "hot and cold" game to the lamp getting knocked over and you losing TV privileges for a week.
Ricky:	Well, I was looking for the remote for a while, and I was starting to get really mad because every time I started to get close to finding it, Austin would change his "hot" to a "cold," and then he'd laugh harder. It was so frustrating, and I knew the show was going to start, and I love the music at the beginning, and ugh! I just lost it. I threw one of the pillows at Austin and called him an ass. He gave me the finger. I was trying to move the ottoman to look underneath it, but I guess I was so mad that I kicked it harder than I thought, and it flipped over. Austin started yelling that I was going to get in big trouble, so I threw another pillow at him. It bounced off of him and knocked the lamp over. That's exactly when Dad walked in and started yelling at me! He didn't even say anything to Austin.
Mother:	What was Austin doing when Dad walked in?
Ricky:	Sitting on the sofa, laughing at me.

Mother: So, Dad walked in the room, saw the ottoman tipped over and the lamp on the ground, and yelled at you. What did he say?

Ricky: He asked me what was going on.

Mother: What did you say?

Ricky: I said that I was going to kill Austin if he didn't let me watch my show. That's when Dad said that watching TV wasn't an option for me and that I wouldn't be allowed to watch anything for a week.

Mother: Did you tell him what had happened and why you were feeling so upset?

Ricky: No. I was too mad to explain. I just wanted to find that stupid remote and make Austin shut up.

Mother: OK. Let me make sure I have all of this so far. You told me that you and Austin were both in the family room. You were just about to start watching your show when you put the remote down to go to the bathroom. Where did you put it?

Ricky: I put it right on the arm of the sofa, and I told Austin to keep his hands off of it because I know he always tries to hide it from me.

Mother: Oh, so you told Austin not to take it.

Ricky: Yeah.

Mother: But he took it anyway.

Ricky: Yeah.

Mother.	I see. OK. So, you went to the bathroom, and when you came back, the remote was not where you left it. Do you remember what you were thinking when you realized it was gone?
Ricky:	I was thinking that I should have taken it with me to the bathroom and not have trusted Austin because he is always pulling pranks on me like this. He knows it makes me so mad!
Mother:	So, you were thinking that Austin does this stuff to you all of the time because he knows it makes you mad.
Ricky:	Right.
Mother:	And did it work? Were you feeling mad?
Ricky:	Yes! Because I was missing my show!
Mother:	OK. That's important. Let's come back to that part. So, then he started giving you clues about where the remote was, and you started looking for it, right?
Ricky:	Right. But his clues made no sense.
Mother:	His clues made no sense, and he was laughing at you. That's when you threw the first pillow and kicked the ottoman. All of that noise probably got Dad's attention, and he came in the room just went the lamp got knocked over by the pillow. Sound right?
Ricky:	Pretty much.
Mother:	So, Dad asked you to explain what had happened, but you were still really focused on finding the remote. You just told him you were going to kill Austin. That's when things got even worse, and you lost TV for the week?

Ricky: And all that happened to Austin was that he got sent to his room. I'm always the one who gets in trouble, and it's always his fault!

Mother: You are right that a lot of this seems like a pattern you've been in before with your brother, doesn't it?

Ricky: Every time with him! He always gets me in trouble.

Step 3: Understand the problem—recognize that Ricky was set up by his older brother, Austin.

Mother: Say that again?

Ricky: He does this kind of stuff all of the time. He always gets me in trouble.

Mother: You know, I think you are on to something really important when you say that, Ricky.

Ricky: What do you mean?

Mother: Well, if this is something that you know happens a lot with Austin, then it seems to me that maybe we could figure out a way to prevent it.

Ricky: Yeah. By you and Dad making a rule that he is not allowed to touch the remote anymore?

Mother: Well, that's one possibility, but I have a different idea that might put the control more in your hands.

Ricky: What do you mean?

Mother: Let's think about what you told me a few minutes ago. You said that when you got back from going to the bathroom, you knew right away that Austin hid the remote because you said he does that to you all of the time.

Ricky: He does. I told you, this is all his fault.

Mother: Ricky, do you have any ideas on why Austin might be doing this stuff to you over and over again—so often that you can even predict it will happen?

Ricky: Because he's a jerk.

Mother: Mmm. Why else? You said it before.

Ricky: Because he knows it makes me mad.

Mother: Right! Because he knows it makes you mad. And when he sees you getting mad, does he get mad too?

Ricky: No. He usually just laughs at me.

Mother: Right. Austin seems to kind of enjoy himself when you get mad, doesn't he?

Ricky: Yes! I hate that. When he laughs, it just makes things even worse.

Mother: And then what happens when things get worse?

Ricky: Then I usually end up getting more mad and doing something dumb like yelling or throwing the pillows and breaking stuff.

Mother: Exactly.

Ricky: And it's his fault.

Mother: Well, he certainly does seem to be pulling the strings here.

Ricky: What do you mean?

Mother: Well, when you tell me that Austin does things to you, like hiding the remote control, and you get upset, it makes me think that he is sort of like a puppeteer who is pulling on strings and controlling the moves of a puppet. Do you know who the puppet would be?

Ricky: Probably me.

Mother: Yes, honey. The puppet would be you. When you allow someone else to control your reactions, you let yourself become his puppet. You give up all of your control to him. I don't think that's a position you really want to be in with your brother, is it?

Ricky: No, but shouldn't he be in trouble for making me do things?

Mother: Ricky, I am going to have a talk with your brother about his behavior and the way he plays pranks on you that get you upset. I'm not OK with him doing things on purpose just to get you mad. But here's the really important part of all of this. Are you listening closely to what you need to know in all of this?

Ricky: Yeah.

Mother: What you need to know is that Austin can only control you if you allow him to control you. Getting mad is a choice. Yelling and

	throwing things is also a choice. I know that your feelings get really strong and that sometimes it's a challenge for you to control your anger, but I also know that you have the strength and the smarts to resist letting Austin pull your strings in situations like these. You told me that, before you even went to the bathroom, you thought he might take the remote, which was why you put it in the armrest and warned him not to touch it. In other words, you could predict that he would do something to tease you and try to make you mad, right?
Ricky:	I guess.
Mother:	What I want you to remember is that if you can predict it, you can prevent it. When you know that your brother—or anyone else—is likely to do something that will make you mad, you can make a choice not to react in the way he wants you to. You have the power and the control over your own behaviors to resist his manipulation. You are lot stronger than you think.

Step 4: Teach Ricky skills for how to avoid being set up and manipulated by others.

Ricky:	Maybe, but what am I supposed to do when he won't give me the remote control back and I know that I am missing my show? How am I supposed to stay calm then?
Mother:	Good questions. Maybe we can make a plan for the next time something like this happens. And we pretty much know that it will happen because, as you said, Austin does this kind of thing to you "all of the time." So, next time Austin hides the remote or does something to get you upset, what can you do differently so that he is not successful in pulling your strings?
Ricky:	I don't know.

Mother:	Let's think about it a little. If you picture him as a puppeteer who is trying to pull your strings, how could you make sure that your arms and legs don't do the things he's trying to get you to do?
Ricky:	Get a pair of scissors and cut the strings!
Mother:	Exactly. So, in real life, how could you cut the imaginary strings that Austin uses to control you?
Ricky:	I could just refuse to do what he expects me to do.
Mother:	Right! So, if he hides a remote control from you, what is he expecting you to do?
Ricky:	Get mad and yell.
Mother:	And so what could you do instead?
Ricky:	Go watch TV in a different room?
Mother:	Great idea!
Ricky:	But what if he follows me into the other room and takes that remote too?
Mother:	You tell me. If he did that, what could you do to stay in control?
Ricky:	Maybe just walk out and act like I had changed my mind about watching TV.
Mother:	I think that's a really good plan, actually. As soon as Austin realizes he can't get a big reaction out of you, he's going to

	get bored, and he's going to stop. This is only entertaining for him when he is successful.
Ricky:	But why does he think it's so funny to make me upset? I don't do that to him!
Mother:	That's a good question, honey. I don't think Austin is a bad person, but I do think he is a pretty typical big brother who likes to see how much he can be in control of his little brother. I'm not saying it's a good thing, and I'm not defending him, but I am saying that there are a lot of people in this world who think it's fun to try to control other people. If we wait on them to change their ways, we're going to be waiting forever! They'll keep doing it as long as they are successful. The only way to get people like that to stop controlling us is to resist giving them the reaction they are looking for. That way, the power stays in our own hands, and we are not giving up all of our power to them. Does that make sense?
Ricky:	Yeah, it makes sense.
Mother:	Think you can give it a try with Austin?
Ricky:	I can try.
Mother:	Now remember, he is used to getting a rise out of you. At this point, he's been doing it for 10 years. And so you are going to have to be really consistent about not giving him the reaction he wants. To be successful, you'll need to imagine yourself cutting the strings every single time you realize he is trying to make you mad. He might not stop pranking you right away, but he'll stop eventually once he realizes that he can no longer control you. What do you think is the best plan for you keeping your reactions under control?

Ricky: Well, walking in to a different room, like I said before.

Mother: Walking away is a great plan. What if we are in the car or at dinner in a restaurant and you can't physically walk away?

Ricky: I guess I can try to ignore him. Or just count to 20 in my head. If you let me, I can pull out my phone and play a game so that I'm not paying attention to him.

Mother: All of those are great plans. And I will try to coach you along and remind you to "cut the strings" when I hear him teasing you, OK? We can work on this together.

Ricky: Maybe you can give me a sign when he's acting like a jerk. Like, move your fingers like scissors to remind me to cut the strings he is using to control me.

Mother: Deal. I love it. Sounds like a perfect plan.

Ricky: Can you tell Dad what we talked about and maybe see if I can watch TV this week?

Mother: I'll tell you what. I will definitely talk to Dad because I think that what you realized today is really important, and Dad and I can both help you try to resist Austin's manipulation. On the other hand, you did throw the pillows that knocked over the lamp, and you did kick the ottoman. Even if it was Austin who instigated the problem by hiding the remote, you are still responsible for your own behaviors, don't you think?

Ricky: I guess.

Mother: The consequence Dad gave you is going to have to stand, but I think you are still leaving this conversation with a really good plan for resisting getting in trouble like this again.

Ricky: Are you going to talk to Austin?

Mother: Yes, I am going to talk to Austin right now. I am going to let him know that I am not OK with him teasing you and being intentionally mean.

Ricky: Don't tell him about the strings thing, though, OK? That's just for me and you and Dad.

Mother: Agreed.

LSCI Skills in Practice

Ricky's mother carefully walks her son through this Set Up conversation, turning what Ricky acknowledges as a typical dynamic between him and his older brother into an opportunity for Ricky to learn about resisting sibling manipulation. The 4-step LSCI process allowed for an insight-oriented conversation in which Ricky realized that he inadvertently gives up control to his brother. It also allowed him to learn strategies to avoid being set up in future situations.

The Set Up can be considered a "gateway" conversation with young people because it often points to the need for a follow-up talk with the person who is doing the manipulation. In this instance, after Ricky's mother has helped her younger son understand how he gives up his control to Austin, she also has an opportunity to help Austin understand that his manipulation of others is unacceptable. The Encouraging Empathy approach is ideal for closing this loop.

Take note of these other key strategies that Ricky's mother uses in this intervention:

- Early on during Step 1, Ricky is fixated on finding the remote control. Note the mother's skill in attending to her son's vital interest without allowing her own agenda to be sidetracked. Rather than shutting down Ricky's preoccupation with the remote, the mom skillfully and compassionately acknowledges his concern ("I know you are very upset about not knowing where the remote is. I promise you, I will help you find it. I'd just like to have a chance for us to talk first. I think it might be easier to find the remote when we are both feeling a little more calm.") while keeping the conversation on track to address the core issue of sibling manipulation.

- Throughout Steps 3 and 4, Ricky's mother makes use of an analogy—that of a puppet master and puppet—to help her son get a very clear understanding of the sometimes hard-to-see dynamic of manipulation. Analogies are often very helpful in a Set Up conversation.

- At no time does the mother make Ricky feel foolish for allowing himself to be manipulated by Austin. To do so would be to provoke further anger and animosity between the boys and possibly set Ricky up to seek revenge on Austin. Instead, the mother keeps the conversation focused on teaching Ricky the skills he needs to resist being manipulated by others.

You don't have to wait for a Set Up crisis to occur in your family in order to teach kids how to resist others' efforts to manipulate and control their behavior:

- Encourage young kids to role-play typical sibling interactions with parents and come up with reliable strategies for maintaining control of their emotions and behaviors.

- Extend the learning to peer conflicts as well. Peer pressure and manipulation is a significant issue in the middle and high school years. Kids who are equipped to resist sibling manipulation at home are better prepared to resist peer pressure in their schools and communities.

- Manipulative people know the difference between someone who will be easily controlled versus someone who will set healthy boundaries and assert his thoughts and feelings. Teach your kids skills for assertive self-expression to fortify them with the ability to recognize and avoid manipulative relationships.

- Pay attention to the stories your kids tell you about the interactions among and between their friends. Whenever the opportunity presents itself, engage them in conversations about how friends make positive behavioral choices and avoid peer pressure and manipulation.

The Six LSCI Interventions

You have now learned how to apply the LSCI 4-step process to six of the most common patterns of challenging behavior among young people. In the final chapter of the book, we offer you our closing thoughts along with some practical tools to help you map out Conflict Cycles with your children, respond to them in ways that validate their emotions and build positive relationships, and establish a plan for how to remain calm when they push your buttons.

CHAPTER 11

PARENTING THE CHALLENGING CHILD
Resources to Help Manage the Challenging Behaviors of Your Children and Adolescents

Through the first 10 chapters of this book, you have learned a comprehensive set of skills you can use to understand and effectively manage the challenging behaviors of your children and adolescents. In this final chapter, we share with you a set of exercises that can help you practice the skills you've learned as you prepare to apply them in daily interactions with your kids.

Just as we started Chapter 1 by talking about the importance of positive relationships in a young person's life, we begin this chapter with an activity that will help you look beyond the surface meaning of your child's emotional statements to respond in ways that validate her feelings and improve your parent–child relationship. Next, we offer you and your child(ren) a practical visual guide for working through problems and bringing an end to the cycles of conflict that damage your relationship. Finally, knowing that parents and caregivers must act as the thermostats of their home and turn down the heat on volatile situations, we invite you to complete a *Personal Plan for Button Pushing* to help you prepare for staying in your rational brain and maintaining your calm, no matter what your child says or does.

Validating Skills

In Chapter 2, you learned the skills of *Drain Off,* including five core ways to listen well to young people. Here, we offer you the opportunity to further develop your ability to validate the emotions behind the words

> Troubled kids don't just have feelings. They are had by their feelings. —Dr. Nicholas J. Long

your child says during a stressful situation. As you may recall, validating is a brain-based strategy that helps move kids from their emotional limbic brain to their language-based neocortex.

A helpful validating statement is one that brings clear language to a child's overwhelming emotions and, as such, helps the young person begin to more rationally process a troubling event. In the activity below:

- The examples in the *left-hand column* represent typical, emotionally charged statements made by children during stressful situations. They are amygdala-driven and not guided by logic or reason.

- The examples in the *center column* represent well-meaning but ultimately unhelpful statements parents and caregivers typically use to respond to kids' emotional outbursts. Although typically intended to reassure young people or set a limit, these neocortex-driven responses fail to acknowledge the distraught person's feelings and therefore make kids feel even more misunderstood, discounted, and upset.

- The *right-hand column* is for you to fill in with validating statements that respectfully acknowledge young people's emotional states, put clear words to their feelings, and effectively help them engage the problem-solving part of their brain.

- The bottom three rows of the worksheet are intentionally left blank so that you can fill in the spaces with typical statements made by kids in your home. If you have older children, this can be a great exercise to do together as you engage kids in a discussion of what kind of language is most validating to them when they are feeling upset.

Validating Skills Activity

Young Person's Statement	Unhelpful Adult Statement	Helpful Validating Statement
I'm such a screwup. I always ruin everything.	It's not a big deal. I'll glue it back together.	
My teacher is so unfair! I hate her.	I'll call her first thing in the morning and tell her what I think of her giving you so much homework.	
I hate you!	Don't you dare speak to me that way. You're grounded.	
You always leave me!	I'll only be gone for an hour. Besides, I've been home with you all day.	
I can't do anything right!	That's not true! You do many things that are right!	
You don't care about me. No one cares about me.	Of course I care about you.	
• Can I have a drink of water? • Can I have an extra blanket? • I'm not tired.	You're just trying to stay up past your bedtime. A child your age needs lots of sleep. Now, get back to bed.	

*An Answer Key for this activity can be found on page 210.

Conflict Cycle Worksheets

Conflict happens. Effective parenting is not marked by the absence of conflict altogether but rather can be achieved, in part, by gaining an understanding of the dynamics of conflict and knowing how to de-escalate problems rather than making them worse.

The Conflict Cycle™ worksheets provided on the pages that follow offer you (and your child) a visual guide to understand—and therefore help prevent—escalating power struggles. Use these worksheets as a tool to look back on and learn from a difficult parent–child interaction.

Directions

1. Select a past incident of conflict between you and your child.

2. Reflect on the series of thoughts, feelings, behaviors, and reactions that grew over time until a conflict broke out.

3. Trace through at least three cycles of the brewing problem situation to understand how events escalated into a no-win power struggle.

4. Use this activity to think about ways you and your child can disengage from no-win conflicts in future situations.

Parenting the Challenging Child • 205

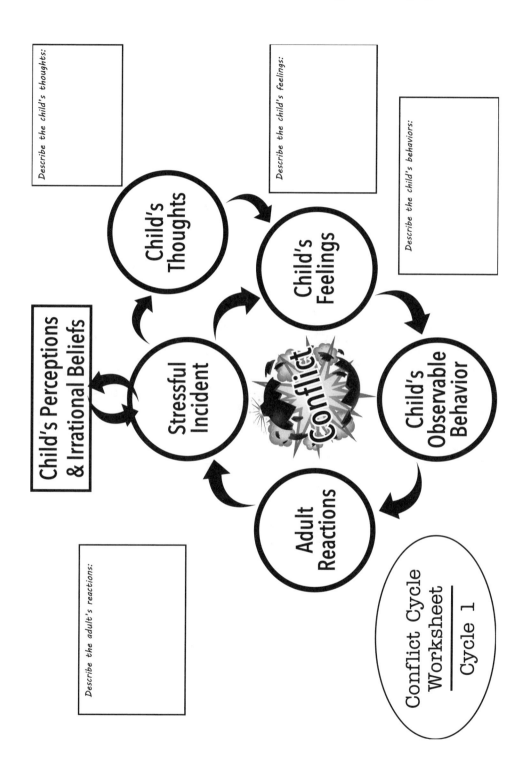

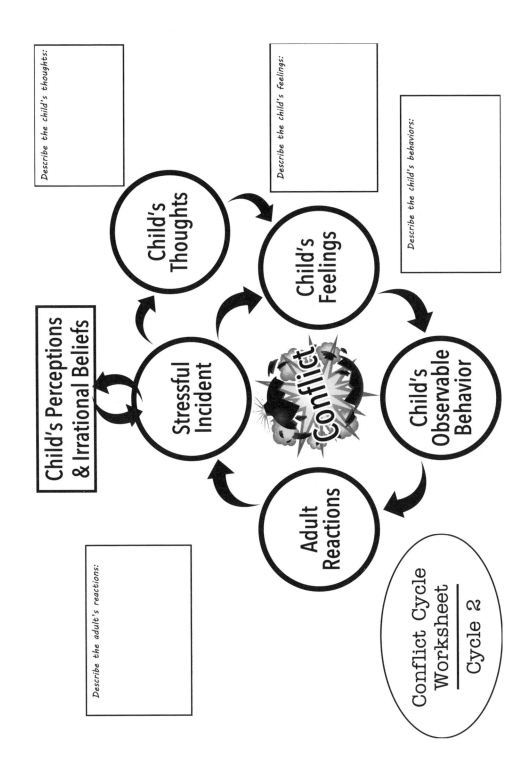

Parenting the Challenging Child • 207

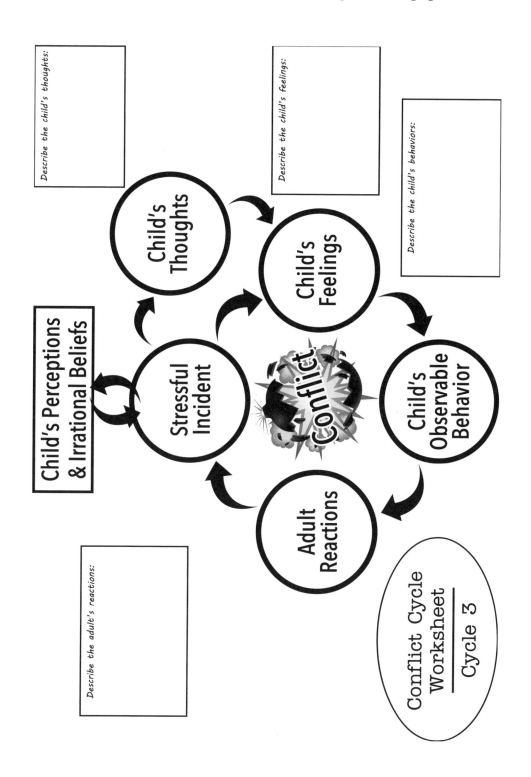

Personal Plan for Button Pushing (Dawson & McBride, 2014)

As you learned in Chapter 1, *your response is the only element of the Conflict Cycle you have any control over*. If your ultimate goal is to de-escalate stressful situations and help your children use the problem-solving part of their brains rather than being driven by raw emotions, you must be their role model of constructive responses to problem behaviors.

Have you ever heard yourself say something along the lines of *"That kid really knows how to push my buttons!"*? Many young people, amateur psychologists in their own right, develop a keen awareness of their parents' vulnerabilities. They seem to know just what to say to trigger our personal issues and instigate an adult meltdown. When we allow kids to control us in this way, however, everyone loses:

- We surrender our moral high ground when we take the low road by lashing out at our kids.
- Despite momentary satisfaction in being able to influence our reactions, young people tend to feel unsafe when their caregivers lose control.
- We miss out on the opportunity to role-model staying calm and controlling our emotions rather than allowing our emotions to control us.

Using the worksheet below, you are invited to make a personal plan for how you will constructively handle the inevitable occasions in which your child pushes your buttons. Using as many rows as you need, identify the following:

- What am I sensitive about?
- What do I think and feel when my child tries to push my buttons?
- What is my typical response?
- How can I change my typical response to de-escalate conflicts rather than fuel them?

Self-awareness helps us control our emotional reactions. In stressful situations with young people, self-awareness enables us to respond (a neocortex action) rather than react (an amygdala function).

Personal Plan for Button Pushing

What am I sensitive about?	What do I THINK and FEEL when my child tries to push my buttons?	What is my typical response?	How can I change my typical response?

Validating Skills Activity
Suggested Responses

NOTE: There are no absolute right or wrong answers to this activity. The statements provided below are suggestions for effective responses that validate a young person's emotional state, effectively decode the real meaning behind the words, and respond in a relationship-building way.

Young Person's Statement	Unhelpful Adult Statement	Helpful Validating Statement
I'm suck a screwup. I always ruin everything.	It's not a big deal. I'll glue it back together.	You are really upset right now about dropping the glass.
My teacher is so unfair! I hate her.	I'll call her first thing in the morning and tell her what I think of her giving you so much homework.	Homework can feel really overwhelming some nights.
I hate you!	Don't you dare speak to me that way. You're grounded.	You are feeling super angry right now. I am here to listen.
You always leave me!	I'll only be gone for an hour. Besides, I've been home with you all day.	It makes you sad to have to stay home with the babysitter.
I can't do anything right!	That's not true! You do many things that are right!	It must feel frustrating to feel like you never do anything right.
You don't care about me. No one cares about me.	Of course I care about you.	It's very lonely to feel like no one cares about you.
• Can I have a drink of water? • Can I have an extra blanket? • I'm not tired.	You're just trying to stay up past your bedtime. A child your age needs lots of sleep. Now, get back to bed.	It seems like something is keeping you from being able to fall asleep. Is there something on your mind?

REFERENCES

Ackerman C. (2018, July 3). What is self-regulation? Definition, theory + 95 skills and strategies. *Positive Psychology Program*. Retrieved from https://positivepsychologyprogram.com/self-regulation/

Baars, B. J., & Gage, N. M. (2010). *Cognition, brain, and consciousness: Introduction to cognitive neuroscience*, 2nd ed. Waltham, MA: Academic Press.

Bell, A. L. (2016, September 28). What is self-regulation and why is it so important? *Good Therapy Blog*. Retrieved from https://www.goodtherapy.org/blog/what-is-self-regulation-why-is-it-so-important-0928165

Comer, J. (1995). Lecture. Education Service Center, Region IV, Houston, TX.

Conceptual hand drawn illustration of puppet (Illustration). Retrieved February 7, 2019, from: https://www.shutterstock.com/image-illustration/conceptual-hand-drawn-illustration-puppet-392787688

Dahlitz, M. (2016, October 26). The triune brain. *Neuropsychotherapist*. Retrieved from http://www.neuropsychotherapist.com/the-triune-brain/

Daughters and mother (Stock image). (2016). Retrieved February 4, 2019, from: https://www.istockphoto.com/photo/daughters-and-mother-gm545119578-98141371?clarity=false

Dawson, C., & McBride, A. (2014). Personal plan for button pushing. In Fundamentals of behavior support: Tier 1 strategies from life space crisis intervention (p. 44). New York: New York City Department of Education, Special Education Office.

Fecser, F. (2013). Introduction to Life Space Crisis Intervention [Lecture]. Cleveland, OH: Positive Education Program.

Goleman, D. (2005). *Emotional intelligence: Why it can matter more than IQ.* New York: Bantam Books.

Kennedy-Moore, E. (2011, August 18). What are social skills? Helping children become comfortable and competent in social situations. *Psychology Today.* Retrieved from https://www.psychologytoday.com/us/blog/growing-friendships/201108/what-are-social-skills

Komninos A. (DATE). The concept of the triune brain. *Interaction Design Foundation.* Retrieved from https://www.interaction-design.org/literature/article/the-concept-of-the-triune-brain

Long, N., Wood, M., & Fecser, F. (2001). *Life Space Crisis Intervention: Talking with students in conflict,* 2nd ed. Austin, TX: ProED, Inc.

McKnight, M. (2016, November 19). Co-Regulation with students "at-risk"—Calming together. *ACES in Education.* Retrieved from https://www.acesconnection.com/g/aces-in-education/blog/co-regulation-with-students-at-risk-calming-together

Pencil sketch of a medical glass thermometer (Illustration). Retrieved February 4, 2019, from: https://www.shutterstock.com/image-illustration/pencil-sketch-medical-glass-thermometer-287122751

Question mark, Question words vector concept (Vector). Retrieved February 7, 2019, from: https://www.shutterstock.com/image-vector/question-mark-words-vector-concept-243217471

Siegel, D. (2012, February 29). Dr. Daniel Siegel presenting a hand model of the brain. *YouTube.* Retrieved from https://www.youtube.com/watch?v=gm9CIJ74Oxw&t=6s

SOS. grunge vintage sos square stamp. sos stamp (Vector). Retrieved February 7, 2019, from: https://www.shutterstock.com/image-vector/sos-grunge-vintage-square-stamp-508572817

Thorn, A. (2017, September 16). Minced words: Perception becomes reality. *Blog.* Retrieved from http://aramisthorn.blogspot.com/2017/09/minced-words-perception-becomes-reality.html

Triune Brain black and white (Illustration). (2019). Retrieved February 4, 2019, from: https://www.istockphoto.com/vector/triune-brain-black-and-white-gm1124562884-295273027?clarity=false

Two businessmen arguing six and nine (Illustration). (2018). Retrieved February 5, 2019, from: https://www.istockphoto.com/vector/two-businessmen-arguing-six-and-nine-gm1045367694-279746739?clarity=false

Vector hand drawn illustration of basic corkscrew in vintage engraved style on white background (Vector). Retrieved February 4, 2019, from: https://www.shutterstock.com/image-vector/vector-hand-drawn-illustration-basic-corkscrew-662184991

Whitson, S. (2014). *8 keys to ending bullying: Strategies for parents & schools*. New York: W.W. Norton & Co.